THE LAND
OF
THE MESSIAH

Deuteronomy 26:9 . . . a land flowing with milk and honey.

DEDICATION

I am grateful to God for the people He has placed in my life over these last decades -- who encouraged me, challenged me, exhorted me, led me, believed in me, and supported me -- too many to mention and they know who they are. Among them, my parents for bringing me up and teaching me to always be grateful and contented with what I have.

My church of origin in Venezuela -- Las Acacias, for commissioning and sending me as a missionary on board the Logos II (operated by OM). Belfast Bible College for granting me full scholarship. My friends in Northern Ireland for supporting me to get my B.A. in Israel College of the Bible. Maoz Israel and my then local congregation in Ma'ale Adumim for supporting my studies to get my license as tour guide and pursuing my M.A. in Archaeology in the University of the Holy Land.

My three adorable children for always trusting and believing in me and my sweet and lovely wife, Wea, who always reminds me to be grateful for what I have but to continue to pursue the best -- for their amazing support and encouragement.

Pilgrims, visitors and tourists who inspired me to publish this book. Remember that by coming to the Land of the Messiah, you form part of a long chain of millions who have come before you and who will come after you.

To you all I dedicate this book, which I was able to produce after over four years of traveling around this fascinating Land, with much effort and challenges.
With confidence, I can say there is no other place on Earth like the Land of the Messiah -- still flowing with much milk and honey.

In Messiah,
Marcos Enrique Ruiz Rivero II (AVIEL)

THE ARCHAEOLOGICAL CHRONOLOGY OF THE LAND OF THE MESSIAH

Neolithic (New Stone Age)	8500-4500 BC
Chalcolithic (Copper Age)	4500-3500 BC
Early Bronze Age	3500-2350 BC
Middle Bronze Age	2350-1550 BC
Late Bronze Age	1550-1200 BC
Iron Age	1200-586 BC
Babylonian Period	586-539 BC
Persian Period	539-332 BC
Hellenistic Period	332-153 BC
Hasmoneans	152-63 BC
Roman Period	63 BC-325 AD
(Herod the Great)	37-4 BC
Byzantine Period	325-638 AD
Umayyad Period	638-750 AD
Abbasid Period	750-970 AD
Fatimid Period	970-1071 AD
Seljuq Period	1071-1098 AD
Fatimid Period	1098-1099 AD
Crusader Period	1099-1187 AD
(First Kingdom of Jerusalem)	
Ayyubid Period	1187-1250 AD
(Second Kingdom of Jerusalem)	1187-1291 AD
Mamelukes Period	1250-1517 AD
Ottoman Period	1517-1917 AD

HOW TO USE THE BOOK?

When referring to opening hours and entrance fees to National Parks, Nature and Parks Authority, Churches and others, visit their website since they occasionally change information.

The book is intended to provide the most accurate yet simple information through bullet points with astonishing inland and aerial pictures.

Akko http://www.akko.org.il/en/

Israel Nature and Parks Authority https://www.parks.org.il/en/

Christian Places Outside Jerusalem http://www.cicts.org/

Bethsaida (e-Tell) http://www.kkl-jnf.org/

Eilat https://eilat.city/en/list/attractions

Yardenit https://www.yardenit.com/

Ancient Katzrin Park http://visitkatsrin.org.il/

Rosh Hanikra is under Akko Website

Ancient Shiloh http://www.myheartland.co.il/ancient-shiloh/

Timna Park http://www.parktimna.co.il/en/

I am grateful to all those who assisted in reviewing this book especially to Catherine Sommer

Disigned by:

Communicoach service.

https://COMMUNICOACH.CA/

ISBN : 978-965-7747-17-9

Written, Photographed, Edited and Published by:

Marcos Enrique Ruiz Rivero II (AVIEL)

Mobile +972(0)546711141

E-Mail israelsuperguide@gmail.com

Website www.israelsuperguide.com

   ISRAEL SUPERGUIDE

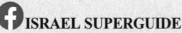 **@ISRAELSUPERGUIDE**

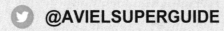 **@AVIELSUPERGUIDE**

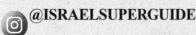 **AVIEL ISRAEL SUPERGUIDE**
tripadvisor

AVIEL
ISRAEL SUPERGUIDE

CONTENTS

Akko 1

Aphek (Antipatris) 4

Apollonia 6

Arbel 7

Ashdod 8

Ashkelon 10

Avdat 12

Banias 14

Bar'Am Synagogue 16

Beit Alpha 17

Beit Guvrin & Maresha 18

Beit She'an 20

Beit She'arim 22

Beit Shemesh 23

Belvoir (Kochav HaYarden) 24

Bethel 26

Bethlehem 28

Bethsaida (E-Tell) 31

Caesarea Maritima 33

Capernaum 36

Chorazin 38

Eilat 40

Ein Gedi 42

Emmaus (Nicopolis) 44

Gamla 45

Gath (Tel-Tsafit) 47

Gezer 48

Haifa 50

Hamat Tiberias 52

Hazor 53

Herodium 55

Hula 57

Jacob's Well 59

Jaffa 61

Jericho 63

Jordan River (Qasr-Al-Yahud 66

Jordan River (Yardenit) 68

Kafr Kanna (Cana) 69

Katzrin 71

Kursi 73

Lachish 75

Lod 77

Ma'ayan Harod (Ein Harod) 78

Machpelah (Hebron) 79

Machtesh Ramon 81

Magdala 83

Mamshit 85

Mar Saba Monastery 87

Masada 89

Mazor Mausoleum 92

Megiddo (Tel Megiddo) 93

Migdal Afek Castle 95

Montfort Castle 96

Mount Carmel (Mukhraka) 97

Mount Gerizim 99

Mount of Beatitudes 101

Mount Tabor 103

Nahal Taninim 105

Nazareth 106

Nimrod Fortress 109

Qumran 111

Ramla 113

Rosh Hanikra 115

Saint Peter Primacy 116

Sea of Galilee 118

Shiloh 120

Shivta 122

Soreq Cave 124

St. George of Kosiba Monastery 126

Stella Maris Monastery 128

Susita (Hippos) 130

Susya 132

Tabgha 134

Tel Arad 136

Tel Azeka 138

Tel Be'er Sheva 140

Tel Dan 142

Tel Rehov 144

Tel Yizreel 145

Timna Park 146

Yehiam Fortress 149

Zippori 151

INTRODUCTION

Where can I begin to describe you?

You have been inhabited since almost the dawn of human history.

You have witnessed the development of human civilization since its infancy: the hunter, the gatherer, the metal worker, the farmer, and the shepherd -- all these despite your few natural resources. You were not blessed with so much affluence such as gold, diamonds or even oil, but you have a wealth of history like no other.

There is something about you that has made empire after empire covet you, control you, devastate you, and rebuild you.

You have seen warriors, people groups who came and left, princesses, kings, queens, pharaohs, emperors, prophets, and endless other protagonists. Mighty powers such as the Egyptians, Assyrians, Babylonians, Persians, Greeks, Ptolemies, Seleucids, Romans, Arabs, Crusaders, Ottomans, and many others have controlled you.

Your soil and sky have seen battle after battle, war after war, and your children are yearning for everlasting peace. Your prophets spoke of the coming of a Redeemer, a Prince of Peace -- only then will you enjoy true and everlasting peace…peace within your borders. Then your weapons shall turn into plowshares and pruning hooks and your children will not train for war anymore.

Your deserts, mountains, valleys, and lowlands dress you with the beauty of the Almighty that inspired psalms, poems, and songs written by many artists of olden days and now.

You yielded two significant faiths to humanity, changing the course of human civilization.

The most extraordinary Man who ever lived on the face of this earth came from within you. With humble beginnings but destined to change the course of human history. He was so special that from His birth to adulthood, His enemies did not accept His existence. He never wrote a book, but countless books have been written about Him like no other human being.

A prophet, a liar, a lunatic, a teacher, or a Messiah? It is for you to decide…

You have been known by many names -- Canaan, Retjenu, The Land of Milk and Honey, the Promised Land, Kingdom of Israel, Eber-Nari, Judea, Zion, Siria-Palestina, Land Bridge, The Holy Land, Kingdom of Jerusalem, Palestine, The Levant, State of Israel, you are indeed THE LAND OF THE MESSIAH.

The book has a video complement via my channel Israel Superguide containing videos from the air for most sites, check out play list: The Land of the Messiah. Do not forget to subscribe, share with others, and like.

AVIEL
ISRAEL SUPERGUIDE

YouTube VIDEO COMPLEMENT VIA MY CHANNEL:
ISRAEL SUPERGUIDE

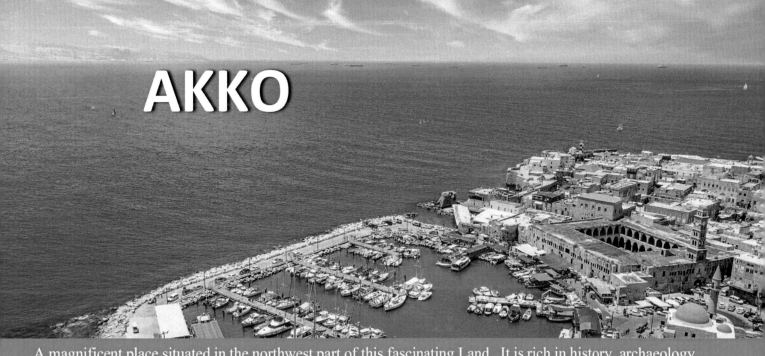

AKKO

A magnificent place situated in the northwest part of this fascinating Land. It is rich in history, archaeology, attractions and much more.

After the fall of the First Kingdom of Jerusalem in 1187, Akko played an important role in the 13th C AD when it became the capital of the Second Crusader Kingdom of Jerusalem. It was rediscovered in the 20th C AD and inscribed in the UNESCO World Heritage list in our time.

Akko, in history, was mentioned in the Egyptian records during the first campaign of Thutmose III to the Southern Levant.

During the partition of the land among the ancient Hebrews, Akko was allotted to the tribe of Asher which it failed to possess (Judges 1:31).

Later on, King Solomon gave the land to King Hiram of Tyre as payment for his service (1 Kings 9:11-13), and it was conquered in the 8th C BC and in 333 BC by the Assyrians and Alexander the Great, respectively.

Thereafter, the city passed from conquerors to conquerors during the time of the Ptolemies, Seleucids, the Romans, Herod the Great and others.

Although in the 2nd C AD, Christianity was not yet legalized anywhere in the Roman Empire, the city had its own bishop.

During the Byzantine period in the Levant (4th-7th C AD), the city had a large Samaritan population, however by the 7th C AD the city had suffered major upheavals.

First, the Persian invasion that lasted 14 years (614-628 AD) and a few years later, the Arab invasion (636 AD) establishing a Muslim city.

It is in the 12th-13th C AD that Akko became the major city that we can see today. It was first conquered by European Christians (Latin) in 1104 AD to become a major port for trading. Led by An-Nasir Salah ad-Din (Saladin) in 1187 AD, they were defeated in the Horns of Hattin (near the Kinneret Lake) and re-conquered by the legendary Richard the Lionheart in 1191 AD.

Akko became the last Crusader stronghold in 1291 AD when it was defeated by the Mamluks and the city was destroyed.

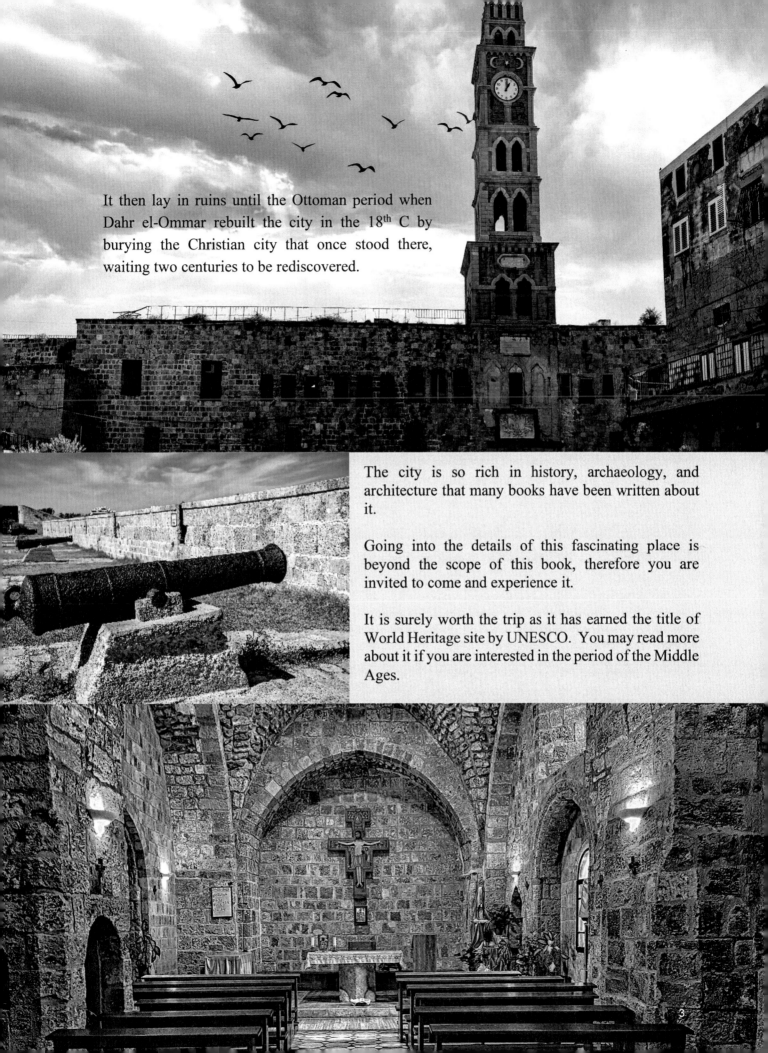

It then lay in ruins until the Ottoman period when Dahr el-Ommar rebuilt the city in the 18th C by burying the Christian city that once stood there, waiting two centuries to be rediscovered.

The city is so rich in history, archaeology, and architecture that many books have been written about it.

Going into the details of this fascinating place is beyond the scope of this book, therefore you are invited to come and experience it.

It is surely worth the trip as it has earned the title of World Heritage site by UNESCO. You may read more about it if you are interested in the period of the Middle Ages.

APHEK
(ANTIPATRIS)

Located in the central district of the country north of Tel Aviv and not to be confused with northern Afek near Akko.

Today Aphek, also known as Tel Aphek or Yarkon National Park, is a beautiful place and very popular among Israelis who love to visit the place for recreation with their families.

Thanks to the springs of Rosh Ha'Ayin, this area is rich in flora and fauna, allowing humans to inhabit the area for thousands of years.

The city is located on the ancient trade route known by the Romans as the Via Maris. It is also mentioned in Egyptian records in the 15th C BC during the campaign of Thutmose III against the local ruler for insurrection in the ancient Levant.

The ancient Philistines camped in the area when they were at war against the Israelites and the Ark of the Covenant was lost (1 Samuel 4:1).

After the 8th C BC, it became the border between Judah and Samaria. Herod the Great rebuilt the city and named it Antipatris in honor of his father.

In New Testament times, Shaul (Paul) made a stopover here on his way to Caesarea Maritima.

The city flourished throughout the Roman period up until the Arab conquest. Due to its strategic location in the Via Maris with access to both Samaria and the Judean Mountains, the Crusaders safeguarded the area by building a fortress (refer to Migdal Afek).

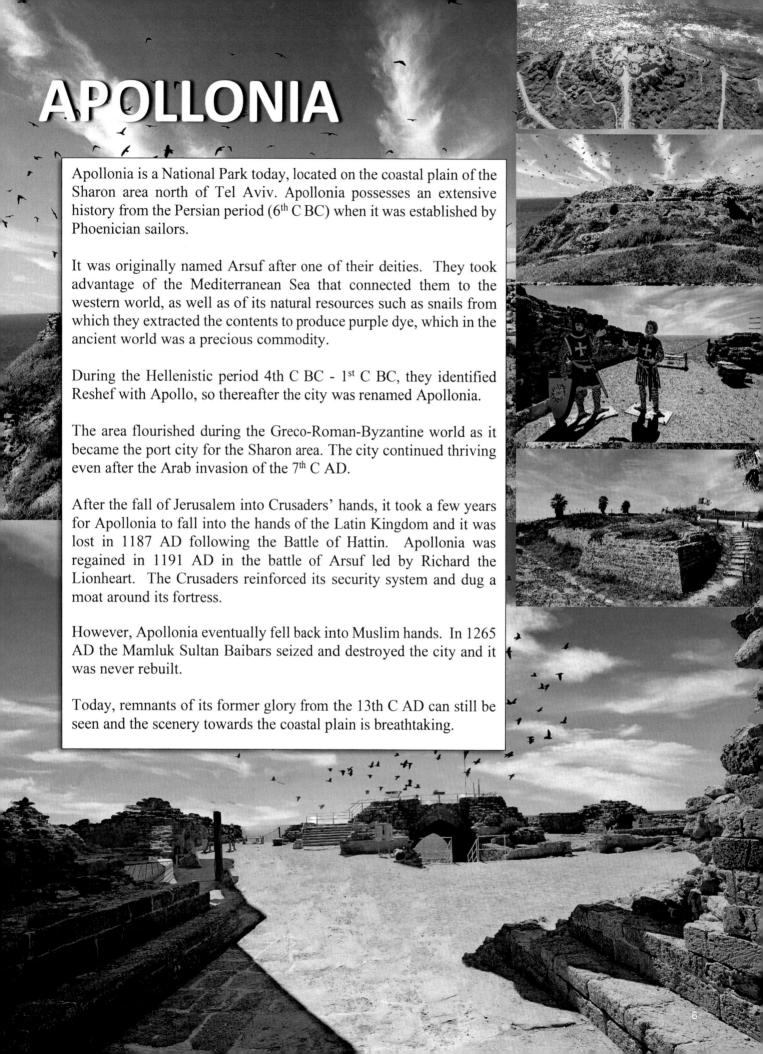

APOLLONIA

Apollonia is a National Park today, located on the coastal plain of the Sharon area north of Tel Aviv. Apollonia possesses an extensive history from the Persian period (6th C BC) when it was established by Phoenician sailors.

It was originally named Arsuf after one of their deities. They took advantage of the Mediterranean Sea that connected them to the western world, as well as of its natural resources such as snails from which they extracted the contents to produce purple dye, which in the ancient world was a precious commodity.

During the Hellenistic period 4th C BC - 1st C BC, they identified Reshef with Apollo, so thereafter the city was renamed Apollonia.

The area flourished during the Greco-Roman-Byzantine world as it became the port city for the Sharon area. The city continued thriving even after the Arab invasion of the 7th C AD.

After the fall of Jerusalem into Crusaders' hands, it took a few years for Apollonia to fall into the hands of the Latin Kingdom and it was lost in 1187 AD following the Battle of Hattin. Apollonia was regained in 1191 AD in the battle of Arsuf led by Richard the Lionheart. The Crusaders reinforced its security system and dug a moat around its fortress.

However, Apollonia eventually fell back into Muslim hands. In 1265 AD the Mamluk Sultan Baibars seized and destroyed the city and it was never rebuilt.

Today, remnants of its former glory from the 13th C AD can still be seen and the scenery towards the coastal plain is breathtaking.

ARBEL

It is a magnificent national park and nature reserve with breathtaking views toward the Kinneret Lake, making it perfect for hiking and a family picnic. Arbel Mountain is located in the south-eastern part of Galilee with so many caves that it resembles a honeycomb.

Due to its strategic location bearing natural defenses, Arbel witnessed many battles such as in 37 BC when Herod the Great came to take control of the area on behalf of his friend, Mark Anthony. Many of the Zealots (rebels who hated Roman occupation) hid themselves in the caves but Herod did not spare them. Jewish historian Josephus Flavius recounted those soldiers were lowered in baskets to quell the rebellion, and some of them chose death by jumping off the cliff. (Josephus, War 1:305, 310).

Flavius himself, who was one of the commanders during the Great Revolt, fortified and used these caves in 66-70 AD to protect them from defeat.

Due to the many confrontations the mountain witnessed, Jewish tradition from as early as the 2nd C AD declared that a major fierce battle would take place in the area before the coming of the Messiah, unlike Protestant tradition that pointed to Megiddo or Jezreel Valley.

Below the Arbel is Wadi Haman, a valley that connects the mountain to southern Galilee. This was commonly used during the 1st C AD and was the area where Yeshua and his disciples passed by as He was going around Galilee teaching in their synagogues -- possibly in Migdal (Magdala) and Kinneret, among others (Matthew 4:23).

ASHDOD

Before the ancient Philistines ever arrived in the Southern Levant, Ashdod was a prosperous port in the coastal plain. Thousands of sea shells were found here, substantiating the dyeing industry during this period.

The city was given to the tribe of Judah but there is no evidence that it was ever in their possession. Rather, after the Philistines failed to settle in Egypt and were defeated by Ramses III 12th C BC, Ashdod became one of the philistine's pentapolis mentioned in the Bible.

One of the best-known stories about Ashdod is when the Ark of the Covenant was brought there and placed in its Dagon temple as the fourth stop (I Samuel 5:1-7; 6:17).

Eventually, the city was destroyed by King Uzziah of Judah (2 Chronicles 26:6) and by Sargon II in the 8th C BC.

The city was rebuilt during the Hellenistic period and was renamed Azotus, plundered by the Hasmoneans, and eventually became part of the Roman Empire. For archaeologists, it is a real pity that much of the ancient city does not have easy access nor is there much left, and it has no clear signs to visitors.

However, most of the preserved remains date from the Middle Ages (i.e., Islamic/Crusader) and it is free to visit any time. It is known as Ashdod Yam (sea) and is 2 km south of modern Ashdod. Many of its archaeological treasures are exhibited in the Israel Museum in Jerusalem and among them is the famous Ashdoda, a small seated goddess figurine from the 12th C BC named after the site itself.

ASHKELON

Ashkelon is also located on the Mediterranean Sea. It has been blessed with underground water that has supplied the city through the millennia. Water wells can be seen all over the National Park.

Ashkelon was a very flourishing city during the Middle Bronze Age. Its impressive mud brick arch testifies to the sophistication of its architects during that period, along with the arch in Tel Dan -- making them the oldest arches in the world.

It was also mentioned in the Egyptian text the El-Amarna letters (14th C BC) prior to the coming of the Philistines in the 12th C BC. The city became part of the pentapolis as mentioned in the Bible.

It was meant to be under the control of the tribe of Judah but they failed to keep it as their own. It was also mentioned in Judges 14: 19 when Samson killed thirty men from Ashkelon to remove their foreskins as payment to a debt he made. When David heard about the death of King Saul near the mountains of Gilboa, he lamented over it. David made reference to the city and eloquently put it, "how are the mighty fallen!" (2 Samuel 1:17-27). The city went through a long period of occupation from the Middle Bronze Age (Canaanite) 2200-1550 BC all the way to late Muslim period of the 16th C AD and Ottoman period, where it expanded, shrank, was rebuilt and habitation continued.

In the National Park, you can see one of the oldest arches in the world, the Middle Bronze Age fortification with its moat and sophisticated glacis (ramp).

You can also see traces of the Roman-Byzantine periods as well as remnants of the medieval walls. Much can be said of this interesting site but it goes beyond the scope of this book. The idea is to present bullet points about the sites and professionally-taken ground level pictures and aerial photographs.

Today, it is a very popular site among Israelis for camping and picnics with the family, especially children as there are swings in the area.

AVDAT

The Nabatean people were very interesting yet very smart businessmen of the ancient world. They were nomads of Arabian origin who settled in small communities and traded incense, spices and other goods brought into the Arabian Peninsula through the Mediterranean Sea.

However, to accomplish such an enormous and challenging task of trading, they needed to develop a series of fortresses along the trade route for the provision of water, food and accommodation through the long journey in the desert. They collected rainwater in hidden cisterns which was also used for irrigation, plantation, etc.

Slowly but surely, these desert fortresses turned into towns through the peninsula -- the Transjordan and Negev. By the 2nd C BC, they had accumulated vast wealth and they formed a central government ruling from their capital Raqmu, now called Petra. Cities of interest are located in the Negev: Mamshit, Avdat, Shivta, Haluza and Nitzana. However, the best preserved and worth visiting are: Mamshit, Avdat and Shivta.

Today Avdat is run by the National Parks Authority and is a UNESCO World Heritage site. Avdat was founded in the 3rd C BC, situated on the ancient spice route (station # 62) leading all the way to the ancient Port of Gaza where merchandise was sent to the Roman Empire. The city developed during the reign of Oboda II during the 1st C BC, therefore the city was named after him since they saw him as a deity. Nabateans also developed their own way of writing.

The city continued prospering even when it was annexed to the Roman Empire in 106 AD. It now forms part of the Roman route desert system that controls the monopoly of the incense, spices and asphalt from the Dead Sea.

As the Roman Empire became Christian, so did the Nabateans. Their temples were developed into magnificent churches that can be seen today.

Sadly, they were invaded by the Persians in 614-628 AD and were not able to recover, not even during the Muslim conquest in the 7th C AD and slowly their culture and architecture become shadows of the desert.

Things to see are: The Bath House, the Roman Tower, the Winepress, the City Fortress, the Nabatean Temple, the North and South Churches, and the City Caves among others.

BANIAS

Banias is located at the foot of the Hermon Mountain near the borders of present-day Lebanon and Syria. It has one of the rivers that feed into the Jordan River making the area a beautiful nature reserve and perfect for hiking, picnics and sightseeing while enjoying the archaeological remains of the ancient world.

It was known as Baal Hermon. Baal was one of the deities worshipped even before the coming of the Hebrews into the Land that was meant to be given to the tribe of Manasseh (1 Chronicles 5:23).

The area was later conquered by the Assyrians in the 8th C BC, and thereafter every superpower of antiquity took control over the area.

In 198 BC, a fierce battle between the Seleucid Kingdom (north) and the Ptolemies (south) over the control of the Southern Levant took place in the area. Antiochus III defeated Ptolemy IV, thereafter, transforming it into a Hellenistic city and the worship of the god Pan.

The area was later given to Herod the Great to rule over, building more pagan temples for his non-Jewish subjects. After his death one of his sons, Philippus, ruled over, enlarged, and renamed it Caesaria-Philippi in honor of the Caesar.

It became the capital of the region including the Bashan, which is today the Golan Heights.

The city flourished during the Roman period, but temples were destroyed during the Byzantine period. Their stones were re-used to build churches; one example is the remains of a church beside the parking lot where earlier Christians were remembering and honoring the miracle of the woman with a flow of blood (Matthew 9:20-22).

During the Arab invasion in the 7th C AD, the city continued to thrive and changed its name again. Since the Arabic language has no letter "P", they substituted it with the letter "B". Hence, Panias became Banias. Churches were destroyed up to the coming of the Crusaders who controlled the area until the end of the 13th C AD. Thereafter the city declined until the Ottoman period with a small Arab population who knew how to make use of the power of the water by creating a flour mill which is on exhibition today.

The ruins of the palace of Agrippa II can also be visited. Besides the local population today, the site is visited by Protestant Christians because of Peter's famous confession (Matthew 16:13-20) "…when Yeshua came into the area of Caesarea Philippi…," notice that the text does not say He came into the capital during Philip's reign but rather into the area which was a district including the area of the Golan Heights today. Therefore, there was no evidence that Yeshua being a religious Jew would encounter a very pagan city of that time exposing Himself to become ceremonially impure. Nonetheless, the place is there to remember and celebrate this unprecedented confession by Peter and receiving the authority of Yeshua Himself.

BAR'AM SYNAGOGUE

It is an ancient synagogue from the Mishnei-Talmudic period located in Upper Galilee. It was built between the end of the 4th and beginning of the 5th C AD. Like most Galilean synagogues, it faced south towards Jerusalem following an ancient Jewish tradition as old as the 10th C BC (1 Kings 8:30; Daniel 6:10) -- a tradition which is still practiced today when Jews pray in synagogues around the world. The Synagogue was mentioned by travelers from the Middle Ages.

The lintel on the door post of the synagogue bore beautiful reliefs of vines and clusters of grapes, as well as the name of the benefactor, Eleazar son of Yodan.

When visiting the place, do not miss seeing the Maronite church that is still standing there. Until 1948 there was a Maronite community that sadly evacuated the place where their houses were laid in ruins after the War of Israel Independence in 1948. A better view is from the air.

BEIT ALPHA

A very impressive mosaic floor from an ancient synagogue of the 6th C AD was uncovered by members of the Kibbutz Beit Alpha at the foot of the Gilboa Mountains in the decades of the 20th C. Mosaics of this kind were common during this time period, not just among Jews but also Christians and pagans alike.

The mosaic is richly ornamented with animals, fruits, birds, geometric designs, Jewish ritual objects -- the ark, and even a childish representation of the offering of Isaac by his father Abraham (Genesis 22:1-19). However, the most enigmatic representation on the mosaic floor which was in the center were the zodiac symbols with the sun god Helios riding in a chariot drawn by four horses.

This would have been unthinkable a few centuries earlier when the making of images was strictly forbidden. Scholars concluded that such a baffling pagan representation in a holy Jewish setting was simply a decoration and that the zodiac and Helios had lost their true meaning. Others disagreed or doubted their conclusions leaving more questions than answers. Today Beit Alpha Synagogue is under the administration of the National Park Authority.

BEIT GUVRIN & MARESHA

An impressive archaeological site run by the National Park Authority. Located in the Shephelah (lowland) area between the coast and the mountain range.

Maresha, as it was first known, was a city within the tribe of Judah (Joshua 15:44). The area is rich in agriculture and has the advantage of underground caves formed due to the softness of its soil (chalk).

After the Babylonian exile of Judah in 586 BC, the area was filled by Edomites coming from the east and it became Idumea. Sidonians also populated the area leaving behind a very rich necropolis. During the Hasmonean period (after 152-37 BC), Jews forced the population to either convert to Judaism or leave! Many chose to convert and from them came the ancestry of Herod the Great.

Maresha was destroyed by the Persians in 40 BC and was never rebuilt, but the Tel can still be seen today. A new Greco-Roman city was born instead i.e., Beit Guvrin that flourished during the late Roman and Byzantine periods.

The inhabitants of Maresha also took advantage of its soil by digging many caves which were used as store rooms, cisterns, and dovecotes to accommodate their oil presses among other uses.

Beit Guvrin is the only site with an amphitheater built originally for that purpose in the 2nd C AD. All others such as the ones in Caesarea Maritima and Beit She'an had other purposes before. Gladiator games were eventually banned during the Christian era and the amphitheater was turned into a public market. Many churches were also turned into monasteries that thrived in the area.

The city was known as Eleutheropolis (the city of the free). Despite the Arab invasion in the 7th C AD, the area continued to be inhabited up to the time of the Crusaders.

Arab inhabitants quarried the area for centuries creating impressive bell-shaped caves. More than 800 caves were mapped but not all are open to the public.

Due to its strategic location between the coastal plain and the mountain area, the Crusaders established themselves in this impressive fortress that can still be seen today right beside the amphitheater.

BEIT SHE'AN

Another jewel of the ancient world dating as far back as the Chalcolithic period until the Ottoman period. A very strategic place controlling the entrance/exit to the Jezreel Valley and the Jordan Valley.

Because of this, the Egyptians did not waste any time and took it over and placed one of its governors on site.

The site was mentioned during Thutmose III campaigns, as well as in the El-Amarna letters and Pharaoh Seti I excursion into the Levant.

It was given to the half tribe of Manasseh since they were already in the Transjordan. However, the Philistines gained a foothold in the area when they fought against King Saul who lost his life and children at the foot of the Gilboa Mountain and his body was hung on the wall of Beit She'an (1 Samuel 31:7-12).

Eventually, David conquered the city but it was destroyed by the Assyrians in 732 BC led by Tiglath-Pilesser III. Basically, that was the end of the habitation of the Tel, which looks like a hill today but it is layers of thousands of years of habitation.

During the Hellenistic period, people did not live on Tels but below them only. The Greco-Roman city that we can admire today was renamed Nysa-Scythopolis based on the legend of Dionysus, the god of wine whose nurse was buried in the city.

During the Hasmonean period, King John Hyrcanus gave them the same choices as the inhabitants of Maresha -- convert to Judaism or leave. The majority chose to leave and in 63 BC when Pompey took control of the Levant, the residents came back. After which, the city became one of the semi-autonomous cities in the region, forming part of the Decapolis and the only Decapolis city in the western area.

The city flourished during the Roman and Byzantine periods, rich in architecture and entertainment -- bath house, local theater, hippodrome that later became an amphitheater, public toilets, temples, nymphaeum -- the city had everything a city of this magnitude needed in the ancient world.

The city sadly came to an end in 749 AD after a major earthquake tumbled down its magnificent buildings. We can still see their columns lying on the ground since the time of the earthquake.
Today Beit She'an is managed by the National Park Authority.

BEIT SHE'ARIM

It is located in the Jezreel Valley 20 km east of the city of Haifa. It dates back from the Hellenistic period 1st C BC, although Iron Age pottery was found from the site. Its major attraction today is the ancient Jewish necropolis which was cut into the hillsides and the impressive glass-making factory during the Abbasid period 8th C - 10th AD.

The Jews failed in their attempts to get rid of the Romans who destroyed Jerusalem in 70 AD and after the second rebellion in 132-135 AD, thereafter Jerusalem was rebuilt as a pagan Roman City. After the 2nd C AD, the Sanhedrin (maximum spiritual Jewish authority) moved north and Beit She'arim played an important role during this transition where there was no longer a Jewish Temple and animal sacrifices, and rabbis asked, what to do next?

There were many unwritten traditions and laws that were orally passed from one generation to the next until Rabbi Yehudah HaNasi took upon himself the responsibility to compile and codify them. Behold, the Mishna (oral law) was born.

Yehudah HaNasi was buried in Beit She'arim but his tomb was never found. The Mount of Olives was restricted for more Jewish burials, and therefore Beit She'arim became an alternative for many rabbis and elite Jews.
Beit She'arim declined throughout the centuries up to the Middle Ages, to basically become a National Park in the 20th C.

It is also a UNESCO World Heritage site, worth a visit.

BEIT SHEMESH

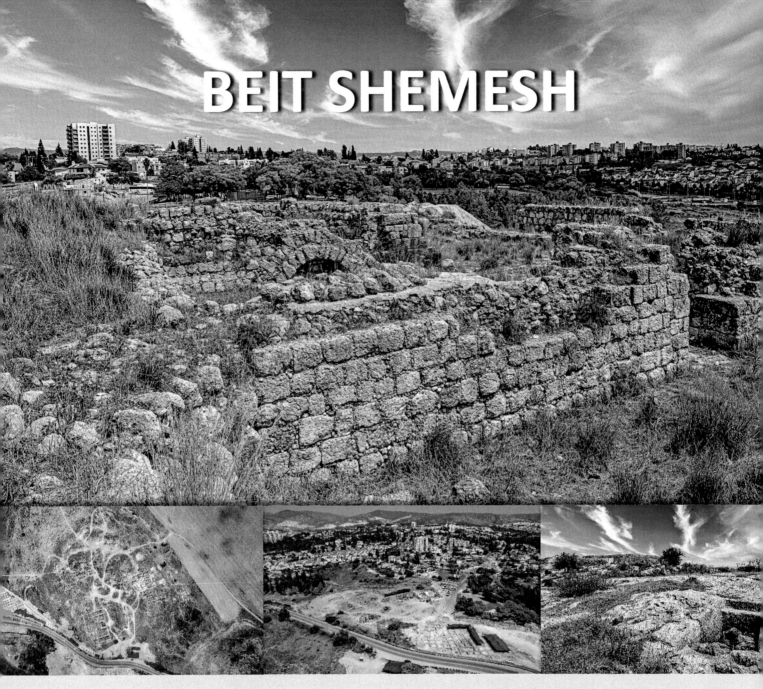

In the ancient world many cities were named after the deity that they worshipped, in this case the sun god -- Beit Shemesh (the house of the sun). It is located between the north and south entrances of the modern city Beit Shemesh. It was a Canaanite city in the lowland (Shephelah) area given to the tribe of Dan. However, as Dan moved north, the tribe of Judah took it over (2 Chronicles 6:59). A well-known story, Beit Shemesh in the 10th C BC, was one of the stops of the Ark of the Covenant after the Philistines captured it months earlier. It made its final stop in Jerusalem when King David brought it there. Recent archaeological excavations have brought to light an expansion of the city after the Assyrian invasion, which was later destroyed during the Babylonian invasion.

Thereafter the city never developed neither during the Hellenistic period nor the Roman period. Nonetheless during the Byzantine period, a monastery was built on top providing shelter for pilgrims passing by. This too came to an end in the 7th C AD because of the Persian invasion. During the Ottoman period, a small Arab village developed nearby which was identified as Ain Shem by the European explorers in the 19th C. In 2015 excavations resumed in the area and as of the writing of this book, new discoveries might be covered up as Road 38 is expanded. Entrance to Beit Shemesh is free of charge. Hopefully in the near future it will be run by the National Park Authority.

BELVOIR

(KOCHAV HAYARDEN)

An impressive Crusader fortress located above the Jordan Valley with a breathtaking view. "Belvoir" means a "beautiful view" in French and "Kochav Hayarden" means the star of the Jordan in Hebrew. It is considered one of the major Crusader fortresses.

It was built in the 12th C AD by the Order of the Knights Hospitaller (Knights of St. John). It has an impressive moat as defense and the stones they quarried were used to build the fortress itself.

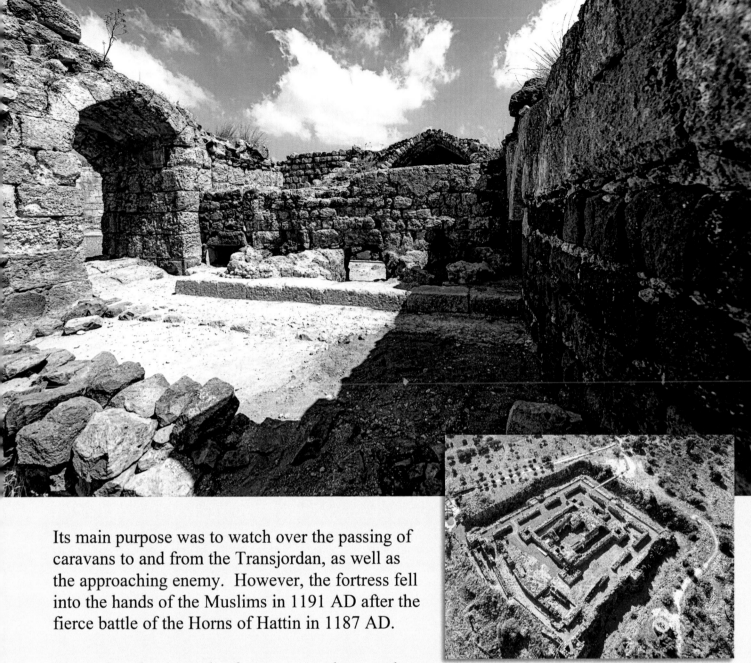

Its main purpose was to watch over the passing of caravans to and from the Transjordan, as well as the approaching enemy. However, the fortress fell into the hands of the Muslims in 1191 AD after the fierce battle of the Horns of Hattin in 1187 AD.

Three decades later the fortress was destroyed, as well as the other Crusader fortresses, preventing them from coming back to the Land of the Messiah.

During the 2nd Temple period, there was a Jewish town named Agrippina, which served as a torch-raising signal of the new month to villages near it. The signal came from the Mount of Olives via Sartaba (Alexandrium) and from there to Hauram.
It is now managed by the National Park Authority.

BETHEL

Locating biblical Bethel as Luz prompted many archaeologists for over a century. Bethel has a connection with biblical Ai, which has also been the subject of a major search (Genesis 12:8; Joshua 7:2).

Most scholars locate ancient Bethel in the Arab village of Beitin which is about 17 km north of Jerusalem. Another suggestion for biblical Bethel is Al-Bireh, which is another Arab town about 15 km north of Jerusalem.

In this book, it is the third suggested location for biblical Bethel (also known as the place of Jacob's dream) by the distinguished geographer Ze'ev Vilnai. This is north of the modern community also known as Bethel (house of God) and is about 20 km north of Jerusalem. Ze'ev not only suggested the place of Jacob's dream but the place for Jeroboam's temple as well.

In this book, it is the third suggested location for biblical Bethel (also known as the place of Jacob's dream) by the distinguished geographer Ze'ev Vilnai. Be that as it may and regardless of its exact location, one thing for sure: Bethel is its central story and the three sites are relatively close to each other. Jacob was running away from his brother Esau and his dream was central to the story of his life. Placing the Patriarchs (Abraham, Isaac and Jacob) in a historical line is not clear or exact, one suggestion was around the 18th C BC (Genesis 28:10-22).

The remarkable promise given to Jacob when he was running for his life was that God reminded him who He was -- the God of his father and grandfather. And He told Jacob not to be afraid because He would take care, bring back and give him and his descendants forever the land where he was standing and accomplish in him what God had promised.

Jacob was astonished at such a dream and, terrified not to take God for granted, nevertheless put the Almighty to the test. Jacob said "if that is so, and if You look after me and protect me and bring me back to this land, then You will be my God" – this indicated that the God of his father was not his own personal God.

Such a promise was never forgotten and indeed Jacob came back with more than when he went to Haram. This story was passed from generation to generation for centuries until it was finally written down and codified.

During the Israelite kingdom, Bethel had another significant role aside from marking the boundaries between Judah and the Kingdom of Israel, but also of rebellion against the central place for worship of God.

King Jeroboam built altars in Dan and Bethel preventing the northern tribes from going up to Jerusalem by providing them with alternatives (1 Kings 12:26-33). This act of rebellion was never forgiven nor forgotten by the writers of the biblical text. King David served as a model king; therefore, Jeroboam became his antithesis.

Bethel also had a connection with both the prophets Elijah and Elisha as they visited the place on their journey before the former was taken up in a whirlwind to heaven (2 Kings 2).

Bethel was also mentioned after the return of the Israelites from the Babylonian exile (Ezra 2:28. Nehemiah 7:32).

During the Middle Ages, a small chapel was built by the Crusaders and later on converted into a Muslim shrine.

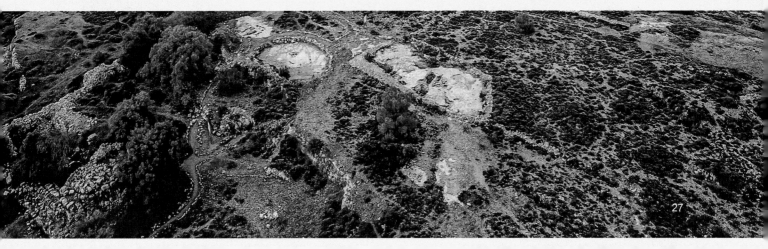

BETHLEHEM

It is located south of Jerusalem and is under the Palestinian Authority, just like Beit Jalah and Beit Sahour nearby. In ancient time it was allocated to the tribe of Judah. According to the Book of Ruth, her and Boaz's story took place in this area. Later on, one of their great-grandchildren, David the shepherd, was born here to be a king.

Despite the Assyrians' threat in the 8th C BC, the prophet Micah gave hope to the people of Bethlehem and promised the coming of a son of David to bring salvation and hope (Micah 5:2). Two centuries later, the prophet Jeremiah reminded the people of Bethlehem that despite the imminent Babylonian captivity, there was still hope for the coming of a son of David to rule the house of Jacob forever. (Jeremiah 33).

Promised by the prophets of long ago and as announced to Mary by the Archangel Gabriel in Nazareth, the super king, the King of kings was humbly born in a manger -- Yeshua the promised Messiah entered into world history to change the course of humanity forever.

To celebrate and remember His humble beginnings, in the 4th C AD Emperor Constantine the Great decreed the building of the Basilica of the Nativity where tradition tells us the manger once stood.

The church has gone through a series of changes and rebuilding such as that done by Emperor Justinian in 6th C AD after the Samaritan revolt damaged the church, as well as the additions made in the 12th C AD by the Crusaders.

Today, it is under the custody of the Greek Orthodox, the Armenians and adjacent church by the Latin Church (St. Catherine).

Much can be said of this rich and fascinating place; however, it goes beyond the scope of this book.

Other places popular among visitors are:

The Milk Grotto

According to Christian tradition, when the holy family fled to Egypt, Mary stopped in this cave to breastfeed baby Yeshua and milk beads dripped to the ground, creating a chalky limestone. Since then, many pilgrims have attributed the miracle of conceiving children to eating dust from this rock.

A church was constructed here during the Byzantine period and rebuilt in the 19th C by the Franciscans.

The Field of the Shepherds

This place commemorates the traditional site where the angels announced to the shepherds the birth of Yeshua in a place not far from where they were.

Thus, a small church was built in the 4th C AD to celebrate this great event. Although it was destroyed, Christians were able to rebuild a monastery in the 6th C AD that lasted until the 10th C AD.

This was among the many places the Franciscans were able to recover and in the 20th C they reconstructed a small chapel designed by Italian architect Antonio Barluzzi.

Visit these places with an authorized tour guide.

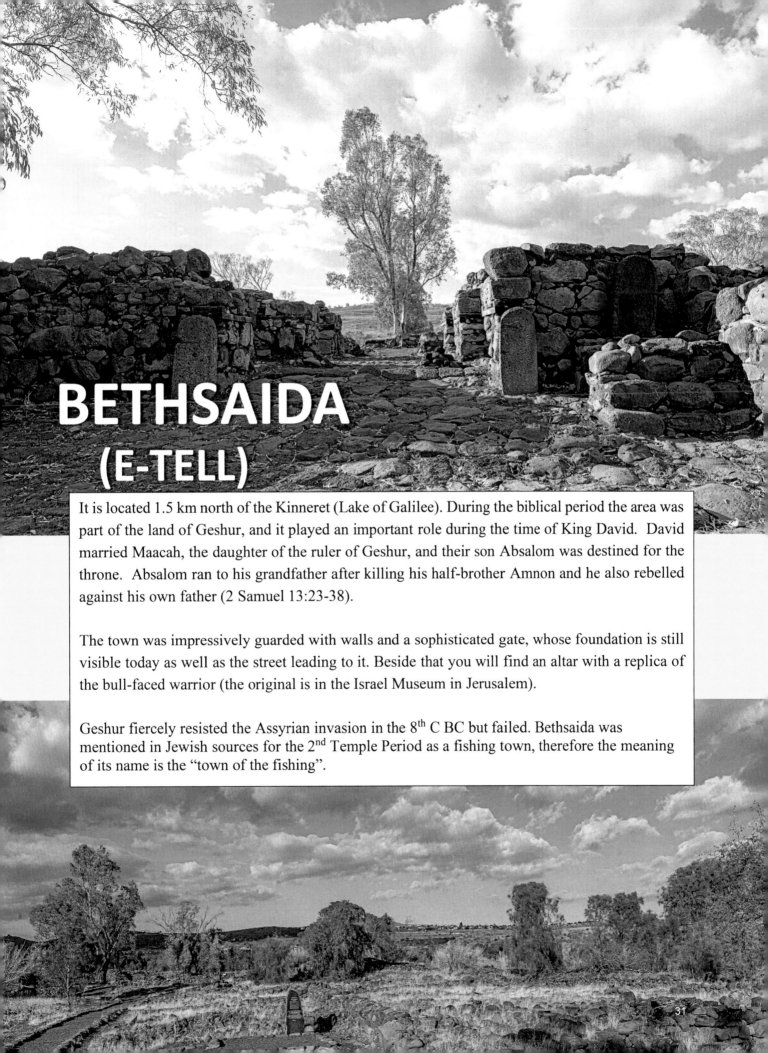

BETHSAIDA
(E-TELL)

It is located 1.5 km north of the Kinneret (Lake of Galilee). During the biblical period the area was part of the land of Geshur, and it played an important role during the time of King David. David married Maacah, the daughter of the ruler of Geshur, and their son Absalom was destined for the throne. Absalom ran to his grandfather after killing his half-brother Amnon and he also rebelled against his own father (2 Samuel 13:23-38).

The town was impressively guarded with walls and a sophisticated gate, whose foundation is still visible today as well as the street leading to it. Beside that you will find an altar with a replica of the bull-faced warrior (the original is in the Israel Museum in Jerusalem).

Geshur fiercely resisted the Assyrian invasion in the 8th C BC but failed. Bethsaida was mentioned in Jewish sources for the 2nd Temple Period as a fishing town, therefore the meaning of its name is the "town of the fishing".

In the New Testament, the village of Bethsaida was where the three disciples of Yeshua came from -- Peter, Andrew and Philip. In Mark 8:22-26, Yeshua healed a blind man and the miracle of the loaves and fishes happened nearby (although today the latter is remembered elsewhere [see Tabgha]).

Sadly, Yeshua condemned Bethsaida because of its unbelief (Matthew 11:21).

Jewish historian Josephus Flavius wrote that Philip, son of Herod the Great, raised the village into a Roman town calling it Julias, named after the wife of the late Emperor Augustus in 30th AD.

Unfortunately, earlier Christians could not identify the town until the 19th C AD when explorer Edward Robinson identified E-Tell as Bethsaida and modern archaeologist in 1987 confirmed Robinson's conclusion.

CAESAREA MARITIMA

This is one of the sites that deserves a book of its own. There is so much history and things to see in this large site that this book will present in bullet points. It was first mentioned by the Jewish historian Josephus Flavius as the Stratos Tower, where Herod the Great challenged nature by building an artificial harbor and using a technology never before seen in the Levant. He used concrete blocks in water by bringing volcanic ashes from Italy.

Herod not only built a harbor but also temples, a theater, hippodrome, bath houses, nymphaeum, aqueducts, as well as his own palace. After his death in 4 BC, Caesarea became the seat of the Roman governor who ruled Judea -- Pontius Pilate, the most well-known governor mentioned in the New Testament who judged and executed Yeshua in Jerusalem. According to the Book of Acts 10, this is the place where the first gentile (non-Jew) and his whole household came to faith in Yeshua.

Despite its pagan setting, there was a Jewish population here who had a conflict with non-Jewish inhabitants. The 1st Jewish rebellion began in 66 AD before it expanded to Galilee and later on to Jerusalem which was destroyed in 70 AD and to Masada in 73 AD. It was in the 2nd rebellion 132-135 AD that the spiritual leader Rabbi Akiva was executed in Caesarea.

Caesarea continued expanding and flourishing not just in the Roman period but also during the Byzantine period, where churches were built and became the seat of the bishop and Church Fathers, among them the church historian Eusebius.

After the Arab invasion of the 7th C AD, the city declined. It was revived in the 12th C AD with the coming of the Crusaders that restored the Byzantine churches and reinforced its defenses, lost in 1187 AD after the Battle of Hattin and finally reclaimed in 1191 AD by Richard the Lionheart. Louis IX reinforced its defenses in 1252 AD but eventually Caesarea fell again into Muslim hands in 1265 and was finally destroyed in 1291 AD with the fall of the 2nd Kingdom of Jerusalem.

By the end of the 19th C AD, the Turks relocated Bosnians in this area and their mosque is still visible today. Their village came to an end in 1948 during the rebirth of the State of Israel.
The site is managed by the National Park Authority.

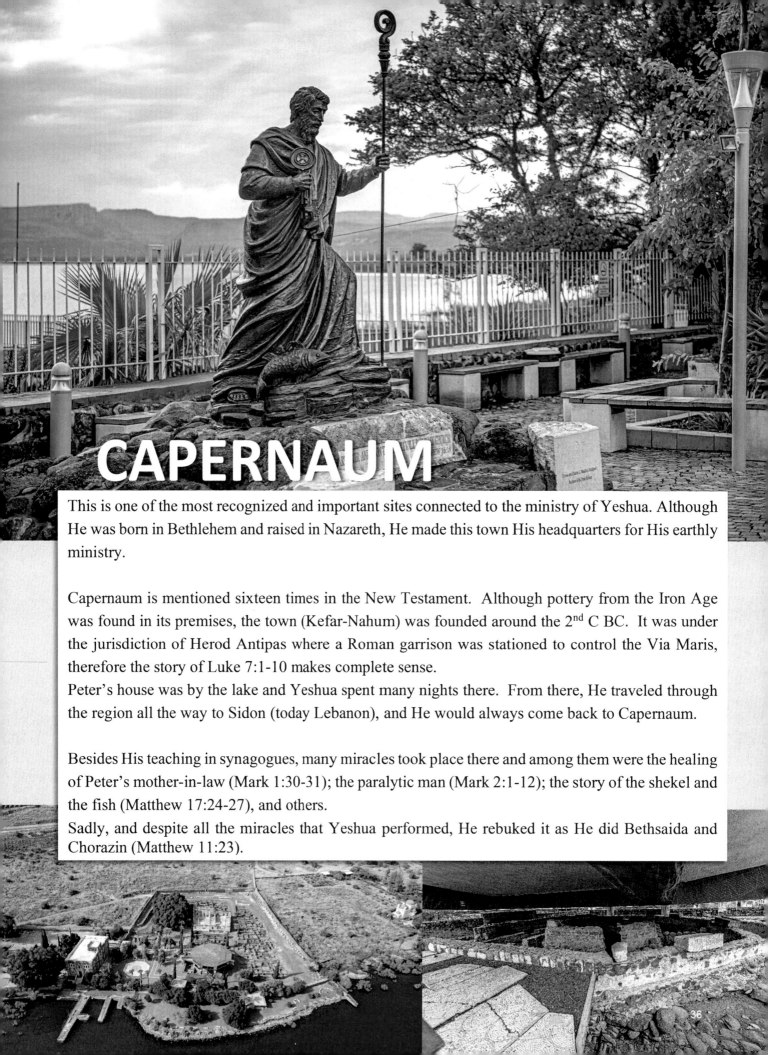

CAPERNAUM

This is one of the most recognized and important sites connected to the ministry of Yeshua. Although He was born in Bethlehem and raised in Nazareth, He made this town His headquarters for His earthly ministry.

Capernaum is mentioned sixteen times in the New Testament. Although pottery from the Iron Age was found in its premises, the town (Kefar-Nahum) was founded around the 2nd C BC. It was under the jurisdiction of Herod Antipas where a Roman garrison was stationed to control the Via Maris, therefore the story of Luke 7:1-10 makes complete sense.

Peter's house was by the lake and Yeshua spent many nights there. From there, He traveled through the region all the way to Sidon (today Lebanon), and He would always come back to Capernaum.

Besides His teaching in synagogues, many miracles took place there and among them were the healing of Peter's mother-in-law (Mark 1:30-31); the paralytic man (Mark 2:1-12); the story of the shekel and the fish (Matthew 17:24-27), and others.

Sadly, and despite all the miracles that Yeshua performed, He rebuked it as He did Bethsaida and Chorazin (Matthew 11:23).

Archaeological remains today indicate that the city continued flourishing during the Roman and Byzantine periods. One house in particular was set apart from the rest as a meeting place as early as the 1st C AD.

Circumstantial evidence and early Christian tradition seem to indicate that the house of Peter was turned first into the meeting place for earlier believers and followers of Yeshua. Later by the 4th C AD this meeting turned into what some scholars assume to be the first ecclesia (church) that expanded in the 5th C AD.

During this period, two communities accommodated the followers of Yeshua and the Jewish community in their synagogue. The synagogue is not from the 1st C AD and is not earlier than the 4th C AD.

After the Persian and Arab invasions in the 7th C AD, the town declined so that by the 12th C AD the Crusaders did not care to rebuild and fortify it.

Thanks to the Franciscans (Catholic order from the 13th C AD) we can now enjoy and visit this place that is significant both in the life of earlier believers of Yeshua as well as its Jewish community.

CHORAZIN

A town built during the 1st C AD though what we see today dates back from a much later period.

One of the Church Fathers, Jerome, in the 4th C AD described the place in ruins (reasons unknown) but the town recovered and was inhabited again.

Local basalt stones were used in its buildings and ancient synagogue, unlike its counterpart in Capernaum that used limestone. Its inhabitants were farmers of wheat and olives. Olive presses are still visible today.

The synagogue is typical of the 4th C AD with a replica of the seat of Moses (displayed now at the Israel Museum in Jerusalem).

This is the only one ever found in the Levant and its earlier reference is in the gospel (Matthew 23:2-3). Its use and significance are all based on conjecture.

Besides the synagogue, there is a ritual bath used in immersion for purification typical of every synagogue. It is called a "mikveh" which is still being used at the present time by orthodox Jews. They gathered the rain water into cisterns then transferred it into the purification pool.

The town survived the Arab invasion in the 7th C AD then later declined. After centuries of abandonment, the village was revived in the 13th C by Bedouins from the north.
Today at the entrance of the National Park, there is the tomb of Sheim Ramadan.

EILAT

It is the farthest southern city in Israel. It is a holiday resort city with many attractions. It is also Israel's third major port giving access to the Indian Ocean and beyond.

The present city was never part of the ancient Israelite kingdom but rather of the ancient port of Aqaba (today in modern Jordan). This has been used since the Iron Age (known in that period as Ezion Geber [1 Kings 9:26-28, 10:22; 1 Kings 22:49-50; 2 Kings 16:6]) until today and gave access to the King's Highway (present day Jordan).

It is well known for its beaches, snorkeling in the Red Sea (in Hebrew it is the Reed Sea), hiking in the Red Canyon, and tax-free port.

Things to see and enjoy: The Coral Beach near Timna Park (refer to Timna Park); Ein Evrona and Doum Palms. If you are a bird lover, there is a second migratory station north of the city. The other one is located in the Hula Valley north of the Kinneret (refer to Hula).

Additionally, the Coral World Underwater Observatory is ideal for children; Windsurfing area; King's city and more.

Ideal visiting period is from November to April as temperatures can climb pretty high (over 30°C or over 90°F).

EIN GEDI

Ein Gedi is an oasis located in the Judean desert overlooking the Dead Sea and is in front of the ancient Moabite settlement. It has been inhabited for over 5000 years due to its natural springs. It was also during this time that copper was starting to be used in the Southern Levant.

This was the setting of the famous refuge of David while he was running from King Saul (1 Samuel 23:29 - 24:22), although archaeology has not found such a stronghold from that time period but rather from an earlier period.

The area was inhabited again from the Hellenistic Period all the way to the Byzantine period. Both historical records and archaeology can testify of a Jewish presence and eventually abandonment in the 6th C AD after a fire. There was also evidence of an Arab village during the Mamluk period 13th -14th C AD but it was abandoned once again until 1949 when a Kibbutz (Communal farming) was established.

It is a perfect area for recreation not just for tourists but also the local population. During your visit you can hike, cool off in its waterfalls, visit the remains of its ancient chalcolithic temple or simply enjoy the flora and fauna of this natural recreational area.

Today, it is managed by the National Park authority.

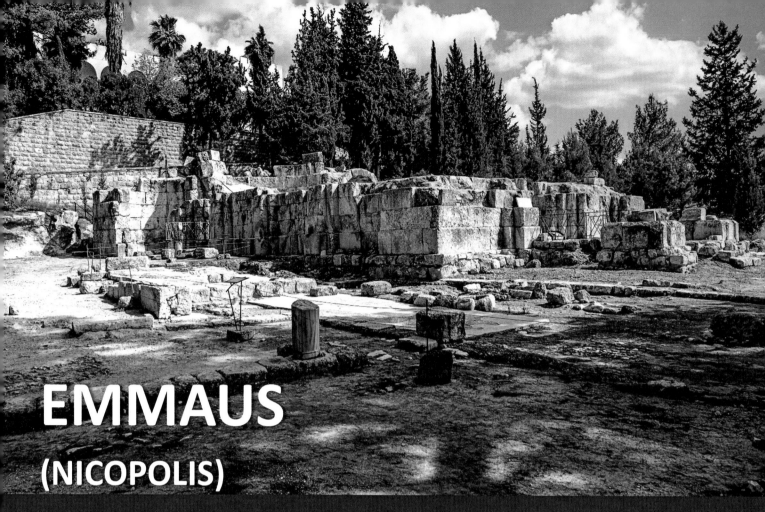

EMMAUS
(NICOPOLIS)

Located in a very strategic area between the coastal plain and Jerusalem. It witnessed great battles such as, but not limited to, the time when Joshua commanded the sun and the moon to be still until his revenge against his enemy (Joshua 10:1-15). In the 2nd C BC, Judas Maccabeus defeated the Seleucid on his way to liberate Jerusalem from the hands of the latter.

The Maccabees then fortified this area which is now located in Latrun Junction. However, this particular site today is just one of the many suggestions for the Emmaus mentioned in the New Testament. After the resurrection, Yeshua appeared to two of his disciples who at first could not tell He was Yeshua. All we know is that this place was a road leading to Jerusalem and the earlier manuscript of the gospel of Luke was not clear about the distance. Other sites in the Land have identified with such tradition, but the oldest was Nicopolis. After 30 AD the Romans destroyed the village, but it was restored during the Byzantine period. It was then renamed Nicopolis or "City of Victory" where churches were built during this time period but did not survive the Persian and Arab invasions in 614–628 AD and 634-638 AD, respectively.

It briefly flourished during the Crusader period then degenerated again after their expulsion from the area. Some surviving Arab Christian villages remained until the Israel War of Independence in 1948 between Israeli and Jordanian troops. Today the archaeological site and the chapel are managed by the Community of the Beatitudes, a Catholic religious order present in the Land since 1975 seeking reconciliation between Jews and Christians.

GAMLA

Gamla is a plateau with basalt stones located in the Golan Heights. It was inhabited during the Bronze Age and the dolmens (table-like structures) testify of their burial systems.

"For it is situated upon a rough ridge of a high mountain, with a kind of neck in the middle: where it begins to ascend, it lengthens itself and declines as much downward before as behind, insomuch that it is like a camel in figure…" (Josephus Flavius - *The Jewish War IV:1).*

Gamla was inhabited again during the reign of Herod the Great in 1st C BC. He settled in the area with the Jewish population who ironically, a few generations later, opposed those whom Herod represented -- Rome!

Through the pages of Josephus Flavius, Gamla is known to us as one of the strongholds against the Romans during the First Revolt. It began in 66 AD at Caesarea Maritima spreading to Galilee, the Golan Heights and up to Jerusalem as far as Masada.

General Vespasian, who later became the Roman Emperor, led three legions of soldiers to end the rebellion.

Apart from its natural cliff, Gamla was fortified by strong walls and towers. However, this did not stop the Romans from achieving their objective of putting an end to the rebellion.

Josephus Flavius wrote that over 9.000 Jewish lives were lost, including the local villages that joined the rebellion and sought refuge within its walls. However, in 67 AD, Gamla fell and was never inhabited again until it was rediscovered in the 20th C. It has now become a nature reserve.

The area was inhabited by a small Christian community during the Byzantine period in the Southern Levant. They also left a shadow of their dwelling and church. It is located near the parking lot and on the way to the vulture observation point.

Highlighted by a magnificent cliff, Gamla has a breathtaking view toward the Kinneret. It is ideal for hiking to enjoy its flora accentuated by beautiful flowers especially during the springtime; many kinds of trees: like almonds, tabor oak, Atlantic pistachio, etc.; fauna: rock hyrax and the famous griffon vulture. It has a bird observatory overlooking the highest waterfall in the Land.

GATH

(TEL TSAFIT)

Gath was one of the Philistine Pentapolis mentioned in the Bible and its significance is found in the biblical text (1 Samuel 6:17). It was responsible for many battles against the Israelites including but not limited to the tribe of Ephraim, killing many of its members (1 Chronicles 7:20-21).

It protected the Via Maris overlooking the southern coastal plain and the inner lowland.

One of its well-known stories was as the fifth stop of the Ark of the Covenant before it was returned to the Israelites (1 Samuel 5:8-9).

One of its most famous inhabitants was the giant warrior Goliath and his family (1 Samuel 17:4, 23 and 2 Samuel 21:18-22). Despite being hostile to Goliath, David sought refuge in Gath when he was fleeing from King Saul. On one occasion David pretended to be mentally ill (1 Samuel 21:10-15) but saw that this trick would not work. He and his men later on became what we call mercenaries to the king of Gath (1 Samuel 27:1-12).

friend Jonathan. Later on, when David became king, he used mercenaries from Gath as his private guards (2 Samuel 15:18-22, 18:2).

Gath continued to be fortified by the kings of Judah (2 Chronicles 11:8) until it was destroyed and rebuilt by both kings of Haram and the Babylonians (2 Kings 12:18).

It was later used during the occupation by the Persians, Romans and even the Crusaders who had their eyes on Ashkelon, which they eventually conquered in 1153 AD.

Today the site is surrounded by local farmers because of its rich soil.

As of the writing of this book, the site remains unsupervised, no public facilities, and the road is rough to access. However, the site provides us with a good view to reminisce about history right at the location of biblical stories. Hopefully in the near future the site will be managed and developed to look better.

GEZER

It is situated in one of the most strategic places in the Southern Levant overlooking the Via Maris to the west and half way to the Judean Mountains. Thutmose III wandered this site in the 15th C BC during his campaign in Retjenu. He then destroyed and took over the control of the area.

Gezer was also mentioned in the El-Amarna letters in the 14th C BC as well as on the Merneptah Stele in the 13th C BC. Although King David chased away the Philistines from overtaking it, he never controlled the area (2 Samuel 5:25).

Eventually an unnamed Pharaoh gave it to King Solomon as a dowry for marrying his daughter (1 Kings 9:16). Later on, King Solomon fortified it as he did in Hazor and Megiddo.

Today we have three outstanding fortified similar gates known by scholars as Solomonic Gates.

After King Solomon's death and the unrest between the tribes, Pharaoh Shishak briefly invaded the ancient kingdom of Israel and destroyed Gezer.

Gezer had such an outstanding view to the coast and control all the way to Jerusalem's fertile land and sophisticated water system. It was eventually destroyed in the 8th C BC by Tiglath-Pileser III and re-inhabited as a fortress during the Maccabean Revolt against the Seleucid in the 2nd C BC.

Gezer yielded what is known today as the Gezer calendar with ancient Hebrew writing -- one of the oldest Hebrew encryptions and is now in the Istanbul Archaeology Museum.

As of the writing of this book, entrance to the site is still free and it is unsupervised with no public facilities.

What to see: The Gezer High Place, the Canaanite Tower, Middle Bronze Gateway, Underground Water System, and Solomonic Gate.

HAIFA

Located in the northern coastal plain, it is one of Israel's main cities and major trading ports, and has cultural and religious diversity. Unlike most cities in Israel, Haifa has a public transportation on Shabbat (Saturday) like Palestinians towns and cities.

The earliest inhabitants of the area were during the Late Bronze Age. Since then, until the modern period, people lived by the coastal area. It was during the 20th C AD that people began dwelling up on the mountain, except for some Christian hermits who lived in caves in the Carmel ridge imitating the prophet Elijah (see Stella Maris).

It never grew to be a major city during the Roman or Byzantine periods. During the Crusader period, it became a small fortified coastal garrison. It never reached the importance of Akko. During the Ottoman period, the city began to develop under the leadership of Sheik Dahr al-Omar Zahar in the 18th C AD and Ibrahim Pasha of Egypt briefly in 1831-1840.

During the 19th C AD, German Christians migrated to Palestine to prepare for the coming of the Messiah since a new century was approaching. Today their colony, the German Colony, can still be seen where many cafes and hotel boutiques can be enjoyed. And the Messiah is yet to come…

Haifa also has the largest and most beautiful garden in the Middle East which is within the property of the Bahá'í World Center. Bahá'í is one of the newest and fastest-growing religions in the world. At the center is the shrine of the Bab (founder of the Bahá'í religion and forerunner of the Bahá'u'lláh). The garden is open to the public at no cost and tours are administered by Bahá'í. Check their website for opening hours.

HAMAT TIBERIAS

It is located on the western shore of the Kinneret and now forms part of the modern city of Tiberias. Since ancient times it has been known for its hot natural springs and their healing attributes. In biblical times it was given to the tribe of Naphtali marking its southern border.

The Romans built a sophisticated spa here that drew many visitors from around the region and beyond. By the time Herod Antipas built Tiberias in the year 20th AD, the Romans already had a lucrative business here. The sites continued being used through Roman-Byzantine periods as well the early Muslim period.

During the Byzantine period, synagogues were built here. Their original mosaic floor which was built in the 4th C AD by Severus and destroyed in the 5th C AD, can still be seen now. The Severus-built Beit Alpha Synagogue had zodiac signs and Helios was shown riding a chariot, hinting at an undoubtedly strong influence of the pagan world of that time period.

Some scholars cannot give satisfactory answers why these observant Jews compromised in the engraving of images which was clearly forbidden in the Torah. Some scholars concluded that it meant nothing but an artistic representation.

The Ottomans in the 18th and 19th C made good use of the hot springs and their facilities are part of the exhibition. Today Hamat Tiberias is managed by the National Park Authority.

HAZOR

It is considered one of the greatest ancient cities dating from the Bronze Age. Its location and connection with the greatest civilization of the ancient world made it the main city among the Canaanite cities. There are basically two major phases of Hazor -- Canaanite Hazor which comprises the lower city, and the upper citadel and the Israelite city which is mainly the upper city.

It is located in the Hula Valley with fertile land and a strategic location controlling the way to Mesopotamia and the kingdom of Mitanni. It was first mentioned historically in Egyptian records -- the Execration Text of the 18th C BC as well the El-Amarna letters of the 14th C BC.

Joshua fought against the king of Hazor and burned the city (Joshua 11:1-13). Certainly, archaeologists can verify that Hazor was burned down, however the debate is still on as to who burned it. Be that as it may, the city became part of the area given to the tribe of Naphtali, therefore the ridge to the west of the city today bears the name Naphtali Ridge. They, however, did not settle there right away since Hazor continued to be a problem to the Israelites (Judges 4:2, 17). It was taken by Barak (Judges 4:23-24) as well as by the army led by Sisera (1 Samuel 12:9).

Hazor eventually fell into the full control of the Israelites that fortified it under the leadership of King Solomon (1 Kings 9:15).

It also underwent renovation that included the building of the water system in the 9th C BC under Ahab's rule.

The city was destroyed in 732 BC by Tiglath-Pileser III and its inhabitants were taken into captivity (2 Kings 15:29). The upper city was used during the Assyrian, Persian and Hellenistic periods.

Historically, the city was last mentioned in Maccabees 11:67. It wrote about the battle between Jonathan Maccabee and Demetrius in 147 BC which took place right by the plains of Hazor.

Things to see: the Canaanite wall; the Canaanite palace; the Solomonic gate, the High place, and the amazing underground water system.

Now called Tel Hazor, it is managed by the National Park Authority.

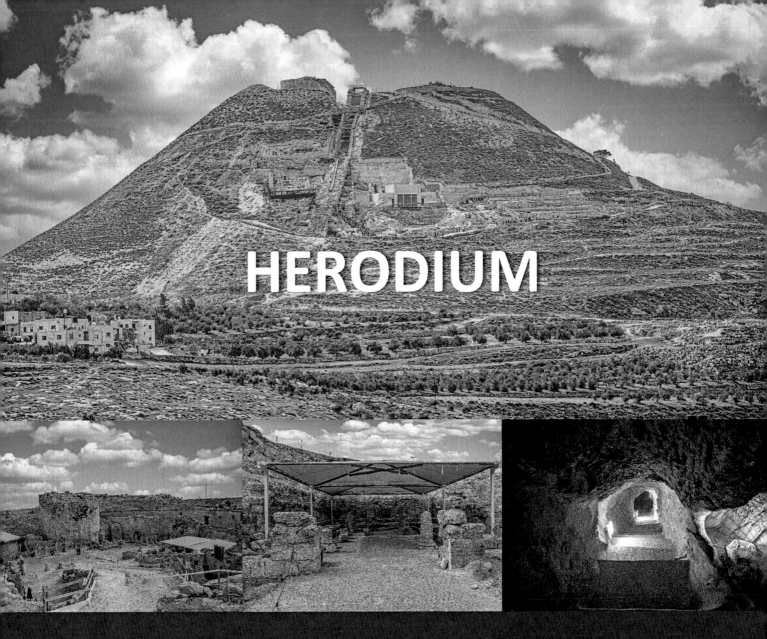

HERODIUM

It is not possible to come to this part of the world and not see or hear at least once about Herod the Great, not only because he has been immortalized in the pages of the Jewish Historian Josephus Flavius, but also through architecture. Herod was a man ahead of his time or a genius by today's standard. It is true he had some psychological issues but it is beyond the scope of this book to explain. You may read the account of Flavius for additional information on this subject.

Herod the Great built masterpieces that were seen for the first time in Judea while others were not even seen in Rome itself. He built a port where there was no natural harbor, flattened a mountain and created an artificial mountain.

That is what Herodium is -- an artificial mountain bearing his own name. However, it is not just a mountain but a palace-fortress complex.

It can be seen from kilometers away and had all the facilities and grandiosity of that time period from bath houses, theater, garden, pools -- you name it, Herod built it right there at the edge of the desert.

Water was a concern during that time but he supplied water via aqueducts. Herod the Great died in 4 BC when the palace was under the jurisdiction of one of his sons, Archelaus. The latter was eventually removed from the position after a few years by the Romans and Judeans when it started to be ruled by governors instead.

Though Herod died in his other palace in Jericho, he chose Herodium as his resting place. This played an important role during the First Revolt which began in 66 AD with the destruction of Jerusalem in 70 AD.

Herodium was taken by the rebels then fell one year later. However, that was not the last time Herodium became a stronghold because rebel history was repeated during the Second Rebellion (132-135 AD).

And this time the new group of rebels circulated within the mountain via the water cisterns which were built under it by digging tunnels to connect one cistern with another. You must not miss the experience of passing through them.

The Romans ended these rebellions and took control of the whole complex. During the Byzantine period, a Christian village was rebuilt at the foot of the mountain with three churches bearing a monastery and a chapel on top.

This eventually came to an end in the 7th C AD with the Persian invasion destroying churches and monasteries. Professor Ehud Netzer from the Hebrew University spent most of his life studying Herod the Great, among many other things.

In 2007, he found a badly damaged but elaborate stone coffin believed to be of Herod the Great. Sadly, the late professor passed away when he fell by the Roman Theater and died as a consequence of the injuries. Today Herodium is managed by the National Park Authority.

HULA

Hula is a nature reserve located north of the Kinneret in the Hula Valley with the Golan Heights to the east and the Naphtali Mountains to the west.

It was once a bird migration paradise during the fall and spring, making this area a land bridge between Europe and Africa. Unfortunately, despite opposition, in 1951 the 15.000 acres of swamp were dried up to produce land for cultivation.

This poor decision in the past resulted in ecological disaster, bringing an end to the existence of varieties of flora and fauna which were only found in that place, and affecting the massive migration of birds that had been taking place for thousands of years.

Years after the Nature Reserve and Park authorities realized the irreversible ecological disaster they had made, they decided to recreate an artificial lake which was a fraction of the original area.

Flora and fauna were then reintroduced and birds started stopping for a rest from their long journey. It is ideal for family, groups and nature lovers. It has a visual center that presents the history of the Nature Reserve and bird migration, a picnic area and a wooden bridge to walk by the lake.

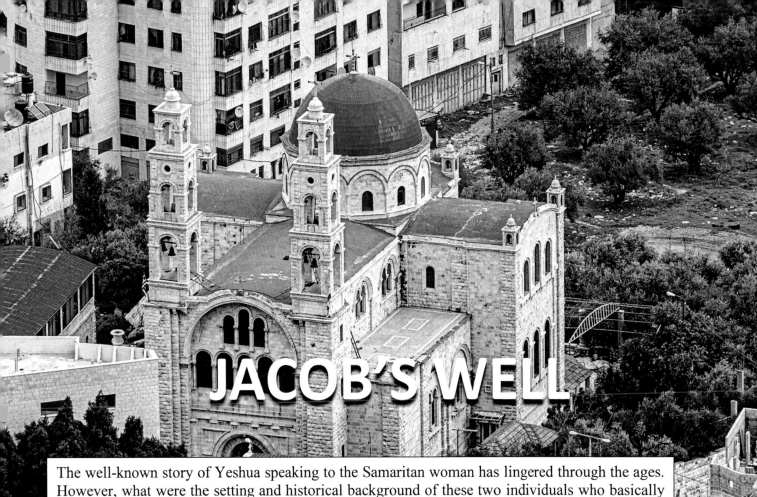

JACOB'S WELL

The well-known story of Yeshua speaking to the Samaritan woman has lingered through the ages. However, what were the setting and historical background of these two individuals who basically did not like each other (see Mount Gerizim)?

Yeshua was sitting by a well waiting for His disciples who had gone to get something to eat. He was bold to ask this woman who was fetching water in the middle of the day, which was customarily done early in the morning before the heat of the day.

At first the woman seemed xenophobic and reminded Yeshua that they must not talk to each other. Then she felt somewhat superior because she had something to draw water with while Yeshua had nothing. Then she cited tradition telling Him that her father Jacob gave the well to the Samaritans, although there were no Samaritans during the time of Jacob.

Yeshua, trying to respect cultural protocol, asked her to bring her husband, not to humiliate her but rather to prove a point. Something must have hinted to Him that she was not a modest woman. She avoided the gossip of the other women and embarrassment by choosing to come all alone in the middle of a hot day.

The woman, in her last attempt and entering into the theological arena, reminded Yeshua that Mount Gerizim was the place of worship and not Jerusalem. Yeshua reminded her that Samaritans did not know what they worship and that salvation is of the Jews -- notice Yeshua did not speak in the singular but in the plural (pronoun) (John 4:22).

Finally, she understood that Yeshua was the one spoken about before by Moses and the prophets as the promised Messiah.

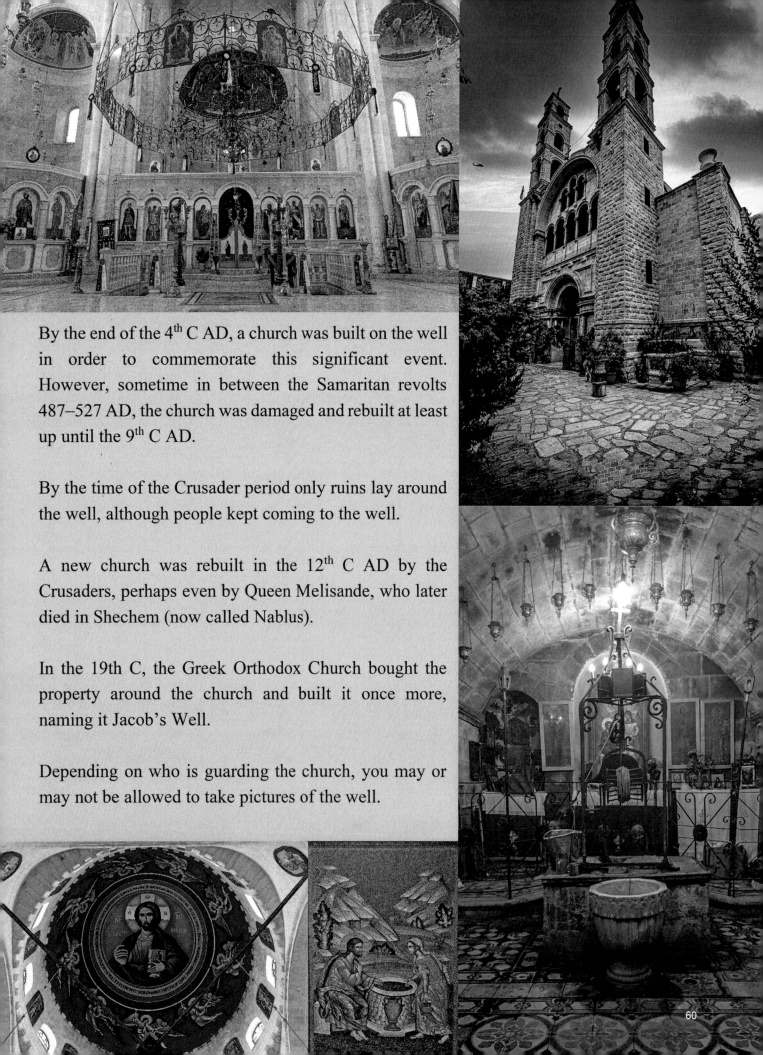

By the end of the 4th C AD, a church was built on the well in order to commemorate this significant event. However, sometime in between the Samaritan revolts 487–527 AD, the church was damaged and rebuilt at least up until the 9th C AD.

By the time of the Crusader period only ruins lay around the well, although people kept coming to the well.

A new church was rebuilt in the 12th C AD by the Crusaders, perhaps even by Queen Melisande, who later died in Shechem (now called Nablus).

In the 19th C, the Greek Orthodox Church bought the property around the church and built it once more, naming it Jacob's Well.

Depending on who is guarding the church, you may or may not be allowed to take pictures of the well.

JAFFA

Also known as Joppa or Yafo, it is an ancient port as old as the city of Jerusalem (see "Jerusalem of Gold" book by same author). Both have been connected through the millennia. In ancient times, it was the closest port to the holy city.

Jaffa was mentioned in the Egyptian Execration Text from the 18th C BC, conquered by Thutmose III in the 15th C BC, and mentioned in the El-Amarna letters as well. Jaffa and Jerusalem were destroyed so many times that their conquerors left footprints on the pages of history as well as in the stones they left behind.

It is located on the coastal plain of the Mediterranean Sea by the ancient Via Maris (Way of the Sea ancient trade route). In ancient time, it was given to the tribe of Dan who did not consider fighting for it, instead they made their way up to the north of the Land (Joshua 19:46).

It was through this port that King Solomon transported the cedar wood from Lebanon to Jerusalem to build the temple (2 Chronicles 2:16).

One of the best-known Bible stories about the Prophet Jonah was connected to this port. God ordered Jonah to go to ancient Nineveh (now called Iraq) but he disobeyed and instead chose to go west to Tarshish and came down to the port of Joppa (Jonah 1:3). Read the rest of the story found in the Bible in the Book bearing his name, Jonah.

Jaffa, like many Judean towns, was controlled by the Assyrians in the 8th C BC and every empire thereafter.

Through the port of Joppa, Ezra also brought the materials needed to rebuild the temple in Jerusalem after it was destroyed by the Babylonians in 586 BC (Ezra 3:7).

Subsequently, Jaffa continued to be used as a port and was taken over by one empire after another, even by Alexander the Great and his successors. It was also part of the Hasmonean kingdom in the 2nd C BC, including that of Herod the Great. However, King Herod decided to invest in another port (see Caesarea Maritima).

One of the well-known stories from the New Testament mentioning the port of Jaffa is in the Book of Acts. Peter, one of the disciples of Yeshua, brought back to life a young girl called Tabitha (Acts 9:36-42).

The most significant New Testament story that happened in Joppa was Peter's vision in Acts 10. For a long time, this story was misinterpreted by streams of Christianity and Judaism, but the text is clear and gives the interpretation itself. It is not about Jewish followers of Yeshua who can now eat unclean food (or non-Kosher food), neither was it about Peter departing from Judaism into a new religion (Christianity). But rather the vision meant that gentiles are welcome into the Kingdom of God and He made no exception between races -- as Paul called them, partakers of Israel's blessings (Ephesian 3:6).

Jaffa was still used during the Roman-Byzantine-Early Muslim eras, as well as during the time of the Crusaders and beyond.

After the Crusaders fell at the end of the 13th C AD, Jaffa was used by the Mamluks as the port for the city of Ramla. During the Ottoman era, churches were rebuilt on top of the ancient Crusader citadel here, such as St. Peter's Church.

Today the city of Jaffa located south of Tel Aviv is a beautiful place to visit -- to walk its narrow alleys, see its ancient ruins, go to its Christian institutions, enjoy its many cafés and restaurants, and of course experience the beautiful view of the sea and the modern city of Tel Aviv.

More can be said about this fascinating ancient port but they are beyond the scope of this book. Discover its galleries and traditional places, among them the house of Simon the Tanner (Acts 10).

JERICHO

The oldest city *Jericho* of the world

Elisha Spring Fountain

This is one of the sites that deserves a book of its own. Its whole history is beyond the scope of this book; hence we shall only cover the most relevant in bullet points. Jericho is considered the lowest (250 meters below sea level) and oldest city (about 10.000 years) in the world. It is located in the Jordan Valley about 10 km north of the Dead Sea and 6 km west of the Jordan River.

The remains of ancient Jericho are known as Tell es-Sultan, a hump of earth with different layers of ancient civilizations. Ever since its major excavations in the 20th C by John Garstang (1930-1936) and Kathleen Kenyon (1952-1956), major disagreements have come up as to whether or not the biblical story of Joshua and Jericho took place here. Garstang argued that it was indeed Jericho but Kenyon regarded this as myth based on the reading of pottery and material culture.

Garstang claimed he found materials from the site from the Late Bronze Age (i.e., the time of Joshua and Judges) but Kenyon argued she did not find anything from the Late Bronze Age since it was already destroyed and abandoned in the Middle Bronze Age.

This argument among scholars has continued until today, the latest excavators of the site as of the writing of this book – Sapienza University of Rome and the Palestinian Department of Antiquities and Cultural Heritage – agree with Kenyon. When visiting the site, it is highly recommended to watch the audio-visual presentation to have a better understanding of this important place. Minimal entrance fees apply.

Jericho in biblical time: seen by Moses from Mount Nebo in the Transjordan (Deuteronomy 34:3); Joshua sent spies into this city (Joshua 2:1-24); the fall of Jericho (Joshua 6:1-25); its king was killed by Joshua (Joshua 10:1, 28, 30); Joshua cursed the city (Joshua 6:26); this curse fulfilled (1 Kings 16:34); the southern border of the tribe of Ephraim and northern border of the tribe of Benjamin; one of the locations of the school of the prophets (2 Kings 2:5); Elisha healed the bitter water (2 Kings 2:19-22); area where the last king of Judah (Zedekiah) was captured by the Babylonians in 586 BC; and rebuilt after the return of the Israelites from Babylon (Ezra 2:34, Nehemiah 3:2).

By the Hellenistic and Roman periods, the city began spreading out. Due to its natural source of water, Jericho became an oasis of this desert. It was known as the city of the palm trees. It was given to Cleopatra of Egypt by her lover Mark Anthony and later sold to King Herod where he built a winter palace. He died here but was laid to rest

After the time of Yeshua, early Christians identified one of the surrounding mountains as the place where He spent forty days and forty nights fasting and praying. Therefore, today the Mount of Temptation has a monastery marking the traditional place of this event. It is owned by the Greek Orthodox Church (Deir al-Qurantal) and was rebuilt in the 19th C AD on the ruins of a previous monastery destroyed in the 7th C AD.

The healing of the blind Bartimaeus and the meeting with the tax collector Zacchaeus also took place in Jericho. According to Josephus Flavius, Jericho was also the city where Levites resided hence the story of the Good Samaritan taught by Yeshua has a historical background (Luke 10:25-37).

Other fascinating sites can be enjoyed today in Jericho: a cable car ride to the Mount of Temptations, different restaurants and souvenir shops.

Despite its destruction by the Romans in the 1st C AD and decline of the Jewish population after the Bar Kokhba revolt in 132-135 AD, it continued to be inhabited during the Roman-Byzantine era all the way up to and beyond the Arab conquest in the 7th C AD.

During the Umayyad Empire, a beautiful palace with incredible architecture and mosaic floors was built not far from Tell es-Sultan. Called Hisham's Palace, it was destroyed after a major earthquake that damaged many towns and cities in the Southern Levant in 749 AD, bringing an end to the Umayyad Empire.

As of the writing of this book, Jericho is under the jurisdiction of the Palestinian Authority and has been classified as area A.

65

JORDAN RIVER
(QASR AL-YEHUD)

It is fed by three major rivers: Dan, Banias and Hasbani (today Lebanon). It feeds the Kinneret and exits through the south making its way to the Judean desert and ends north of the Dead Sea.

Throughout history until today, it has served as a border between tribes, kingdoms and modern countries. Several biblical characters also traversed its waters.

Early Christians commemorated several of the most relevant of these crossovers and events. For instance, the crossing of the Israelites into the Promised Land (Numbers 33:51; 35:10). Its water parted in two as the priests stood while the Ark of the Covenant was carried across (Joshua 3:17).

Centuries later the Prophet Elijah did the same in this river where his departure into heaven in chariots of fire happened (2 Kings 2:6-11).

John was baptizing in the waters of the Jordan, more specifically Bethany beyond the Jordan (John 1:28; 3:26).

The most significant event for early and modern Christians was the baptism of Yeshua by his cousin John in the waters of the Jordan (Matthew 3:13-17). The way Matthew narrated the event tells of the significance of the beginning of the ministry of the Messiah.

The waters parted before the priests carrying the Ark of the Covenant and the prophets Elijah and Elisha, symbolizing that the heavens also parted -- a sign that more than a prophet was present.

Then the voice confirming who was the Messiah (Psalm 2:7) -- "You are my son..." and the Prophet Isaiah on the Servant of the Lord, "Behold my servant, whom I uphold, my chosen, in whom my soul delights..." (Isaiah 42:1).

Such events were remembered and celebrated by billions of Christians during the last two millenniums and many millions more who keep on coming to this water to both celebrate and remember their declaration of their faith before the world.

Churches and monasteries were built on areas near the Jordan River but sadly these were destroyed during the Persian invasion in 614-628 AD.

Despite the destruction, this did not stop Christians from coming to the area throughout the ages, except after the 1948 War of Independence.

The area was in Jordanian hands until 1967 (or Six Day War) so those who came did so through the eastern side of the Jordan.

During this time an alternative site was created up north in the outlet of the Kinneret (see Yardenit).

Since 2011 Christians have been able to come back to the waters of the Jordan in the southern portion before it enters the Dead Sea. Unfortunately, this area is not what it used to be since it has shrunk by roughly 90% in recent times.

Known as Qasr al-Yehud or Baptismal site, it is operated by the National Park Authority.

Entrance is free as of the writing of this book.

JORDAN RIVER
(YARDENIT)

It is located in the southern part of the Kinneret and was created as an alternative for Christians to experience baptism or renew their baptismal vows, since for decades access to Qasr al-Yehud was prohibited due to land mines left by Israel after the war.

Baptism or immersion in waters during the time of Yeshua had a different significance: impurity - prior to going to the temple before the presence of God (nothing to do with sin), a person needed to purify himself; conversion - if a gentile converted to Judaism, one of the steps was immersion in waters; national repentance - Yom Kippur or the Day of Atonement, as a nation the people purified themselves to encounter their Creator; repentance - practiced by John the Baptist, and the only one Christians adopted for themselves.

The first three are still practiced today by orthodox Jews. Note: this time there is no infant baptism or dunking of one another in water (that is a Protestant tradition); early Christians imitated for centuries what was done in the late Second Temple period i.e., immersion in water as (naked) adults.

KAFR KANNA
(CANA)

The Book of John tells us of Yeshua's first miracle of converting water into wine. He, His mother and disciples were invited to a wedding that took place on a Tuesday (third day) – getting married on that day is an ancient Jewish tradition (especially among Orthodox Jews) that still continues today.

During the ceremonies, that normally lasted for a few days (this tradition is still observed today among Bedouins living in the desert), they realized they had run out of wine, and such a situation was a major embarrassment for the organizer and master of ceremonies. Somehow Mary, the mother of Yeshua, got involved: perhaps because she was a close relative? We do not know, but we do know the outcome -- she asked her Son to do something about it. And Mary's command to the servants and for us today is: "do whatever He (Yeshua) tells you to do".

The miracle transpired when the matter (i.e., water) was transformed into a different substance (i.e., wine) and it ended up being a better wine than the one they served first. He did this so His disciples would believe in Him (John 2:1-11). Theologians today suggest that Yeshua being present at the wedding symbolizes that He blesses the union of a man and a woman as the Creator intended it from the beginning. This leads many Christians who come to Kafr Kanna today not just to remember and commemorate the Master's first miracle but also to renew their marriage vows.

However, Cana of Galilee is one of the places that we are not certain of its location. Through the two millenniums, Christians have placed it in different locations. There are at least three candidates.

Before this book unveils the three locations, note that Galilee is not a town or city but a geographical area, which today is divided between Upper Galilee and Lower Galilee. Geographical areas do not mind about political borders, i.e., Upper Galilee today is north of Israel and south of Lebanon.

There is Qana in southern Lebanon (Upper Galilee) where local Christians believe Cana of the Book of John is located. There is Khirbet Kana which is located near the Beth Netofa valley in Lower Galilee, and Kafr Kanna as well in Lower Galilee a few kilometers north of Nazareth.

Qana in Upper Galilee was favored by Eusebius, one of the Church Fathers in the 4th C AD, in his Onomasticon. The pilgrim from Piacenza (circa 570 AD) was most detailed in his visit to Cana which was close to Zepphoris and Nazareth, where Kafr Kanna and Khirbet Kana are today.

Today, Khirbet Kana is favored by scholars and the local Arab Christians of the town, with whom the author of this book had the pleasure of sharing in one of his many trips to the area. Scholars are inclined to accept it based on the actual material culture they found in the ruins of Kana (Khirbet in Arabic means: ruins) and writings from the Medieval period (12th C AD).

Kafr Cana is the most visited so far and is the latest tradition among the three -- the Franciscans acquired the property and the blessing of the Vatican in the 19th C AD, although they were already present in that village centuries earlier. The present church was built in 1881 AD and then amplified in 1897-1905, bringing to light what was beneath the church.

Houses from the 1st- 4th C AD, a synagogue from 4th- 5th C AD, tombs from 5th- 6th C AD (Byzantine), and buildings from the Middle Ages around the 14th C AD can all be seen today when visiting the site.

On the level of the synagogue and mosaic floor were found texts written in Aramaic giving thanks to the donor of the mosaic: "Blessed be the memory of Joseph son of Talhum son of Butah and his sons, who made this picture (i.e., mosaic). Blessings be upon them. "

Today the Church of the First Miracle is under the custody of the Franciscans, visit their website for opening hours or to arrange liturgy or ceremonies.

KATZRIN

Ancient Katzrin was one of the twenty-five Talmudic villages from the 2nd - 8th C AD found in the Golan Heights. It was modestly built using local basalt stones. Like Syria, the main source of income for Katzrin depended on olive oil production and export beyond its border.

Due to the lack of protection along the trade route, an epidemic and a high magnitude earthquake in 749 AD, the village was abandoned. However, during the Mamluk period 14th-15th C AD, a small Muslim community developed in the area. Near the entrance of the park today are the two stone houses used by northern Bedouins who left after the Six Days War of 1967.

In early 1970s the Golan area was scouted yielding many ancient treasures such as the synagogue found in the village, which was partially restored and is one of the best preserved from the Golan Heights.

Local residents invested in the synagogue to have a beautifully decorated edifice as the main public building of the village. The synagogue is also facing the direction of Jerusalem. The building was high enough to be seen throughout the village.

It was used daily for prayers, Torah reading, and discussions. Today it is used for special events such as weddings and Bar Mitzvah (a 13-year-old boy coming to responsibility for his actions before God).

One of the houses restored used to belong to Rabbi Abum. Considered an average house of that period, it had a cooking area, master bedroom on the second floor, living hall that was used to welcome visitors and at night as bedroom for the children, sophisticated ceiling engineering, and a yard used to raise small animals like chickens, goats, and pigeons.

The village was built near a spring where the locals collected their water, washed their clothes and took a bath. Ethnographic studies of the area showed an estimate of seventy families.

Near the synagogue was the market place where business was conducted among the villagers. When going to the site make sure to visit the building with the Talmudic experience right beside the oil press.

KURSI

Yeshua was such an extraordinary man, at times He did or said things that even two millenniums later leave us in awe or still scratching our heads. He was a man who was an observant religious Jew. He was clear of his mission and purpose in life -- to preach and heal the lost sheep of Israel, among others. Yet one time, He told His disciples to get into the boat and cross over to the eastern side of the lake which at that time was populated with gentiles and known as the area of Gergesenes (Matthew 8:23-34).

Actually, even the Talmud (Jewish literature post destruction of the Temple in Jerusalem) testified that Kursi was a center of idol worship and religious observant Jews kept away from those type of places.

Yet we read that Yeshua stepped into that place where He encountered not just regular gentiles (non-Jews) but men who were demon-possessed. They were so strong and scary that people avoided the area. Luke who was not an eyewitness like Mathew, told us it was one demon-possessed man (Luke 8:26-36). Be that as it may, Yeshua stepped into an area that could put Him in danger of defilement or of making Him ritually impure, but it did not.

Both Luke and Matthew tell us that the demons knew exactly who Yeshua was and recognized the power within Him. They begged Him not to torment them before their time and send them to the Abyss (wherever that place was that even demons feared to go) but pleaded with Him to send them instead into a herd of pigs. That was an obvious indication that those around that place were not Jews, since observant Jews then and now do not eat pork.

Somehow Yeshua seemed to have mercy on them, and He commanded them with authority to leave those men in peace and enter into animals that lost control, ran into the lake and drowned. After such an event, those tending the pigs reported to the town what happened and Yeshua became "persona non grata" when He was requested by the people to leave the region.

Why did Yeshua and His disciples cross the lake, exposing themselves to danger and even becoming ceremonially unclean by being in contact with pagans, pigs, dead bodies? We have no answer. We do not hear or read about these men. Perhaps the text teaches us that Yeshua does not only have power over the winds but also over evil spirits.

We do know, however, that early Christians identified present day Kursi as the site of the herd of pigs in the eastern part of the lake, where a church and one of the largest monasteries during the Byzantine period were built. They were, however, destroyed during the Persian invasion 614-628 AD. They were partially reconstructed and later abandoned in the 9th C AD. Since then, Christians have stopped making pilgrimages to the place to remember the power of Yeshua over evil spirits.

The ancient church was built in a style typical of the period (5th C AD) - with an atrium, narthex, main nave and two aisles on each side, apse, and baptistery. It also had an oil press for their use and a city wall.

The site was discovered by accident in 1970 during a road construction and since then the National Park Authority has reconstructed the place and started managing it. It was in 1982 that Christians began visiting the area to remember the power of Yeshua not just over the wind but evil spirits as well.

74

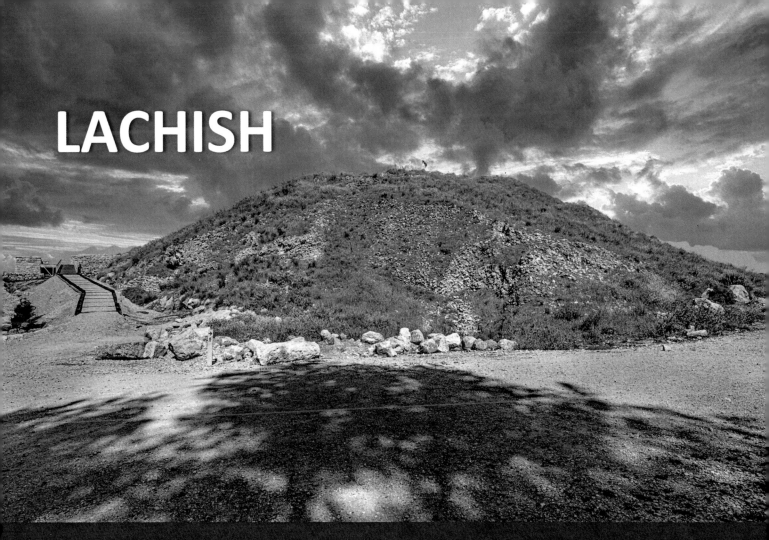

LACHISH

It is located on the lowland (Shephelah), overlooking the coastal plain to the west and mountain of Hebron to the east.

By the time the Hebrews took it, the site had two millenniums of habitation by the Canaanites until the Persian period in the 4ᵗʰ C BC resulting in what is known to archaeologists as Tel or Tell (an artificial hill with layers or strata of different periods of habitation).

Lachish was mentioned in the El-Amarna letters (14ᵗʰ C BC) and the biblical records. Its most well-known record was during the Assyrian invasion led by King Sennacherib in 702-701 BC. He besieged the city and built a ramp to penetrate the fortress and this was recorded in a relief which he exposed in his palace in Nineveh (today Iraq). It is now in the British Museum in London and a replica is in the Israel Museum in Jerusalem.

732 BC marked the invasion of the Land led by the Assyrians under the leadership of Tiglath-Pileser III and later on of Sargon II around 722 BC when some of the people from the northern tribes were deported. As a result of these deportations, the urban legend of the "Ten lost Tribes" was created. Today we know not just based on biblical records but also on Assyrian records and ethnographic studies of the land, that not every person was deported, they took the nobility, high officials but the common people were left behind.

During this time, Judah was left as an Assyrian vassal, however, King Hezekiah and the Philistines rulers decided to rebel against the King of Assyria, bringing upon themselves calamity and destruction.

Lachish was the most important city in Judah besides Jerusalem but it suffered the consequences of poor decisions made by the king. The reliefs showed the fierce battle, Judeans carried captive, the king of Judah kneeling before Sennacherib, and the city plundered including cultic objects.

Lachish was also a cultic center besides the one in Jerusalem, telling us that the so-called Hezekiah "reform" was not as wide-spread as the public presumed, or else the people in Lachish did not get the reform memo from Jerusalem. As of the writing of this book, Lachish continues to be excavated.

It is open to the public and has the only Assyrian ramp in the world. After going to Lachish, it is recommended to visit as well the Israel Museum in Jerusalem to see the replica of the battle of Lachish or Assyrian reliefs or see the original in the British Museum in London.

LOD

Although the city has thousands of years of habitation, this book only concentrates on the last two thousand years.

Lod was mentioned in the Book of Acts and it was known as Lydda that local believers visited (Acts 9:32-34).

In the 3rd C AD, the city was renamed Diospolis (City of God).

It was from this time period when the city was well known among the early Christians, medieval Christians and Eastern Christians. The legendary George, a Roman Christian soldier, was born in the city. He died during the persecution of Christians under Emperor Diocletian (Caesar 284th-305th AD).

By the 5th C AD, he was venerated as a martyr and in the 6th C AD, a church was built on his alleged tomb. St. George became the Saint of Palestine. The church was destroyed during the Persian invasion of 614 AD after Emperor Heraclius lost in 613th AD (in Antioch). Churches and monasteries here were destroyed between 614 and 628 AD. The churches were then repaired and functioned until the first

decade of 11th C AD but were destroyed again by Al-Hakim bi-Amr Allah. During the Crusader kingdom, the church was rebuilt with the figure of St. George, highly esteemed and venerated. The legend of St. George killing or slaying the dragon was born during the Crusader period.

Richard the Lionheart adopted the Red Cross on white background as inspired by St. George, which was taken back to England and Europe. This later became the Red Cross on the flag of England and St. George became the patron saint of England. In the 13th C AD, the church was destroyed again by the Mamluks, then they built a mosque on the ruins of the church.

The present church was built on the previous ruins by the Greek Orthodox Church beside the Al-Omari Mosque. North of St. George's Church are the ruins of Khan el-Hilu (inn), built in the 19th C AD. Northwest from the Khan is an impressive Roman mosaic floor which is closed to the public as of the writing of this book.

MA'AYAN HAROD
(EIN HAROD)

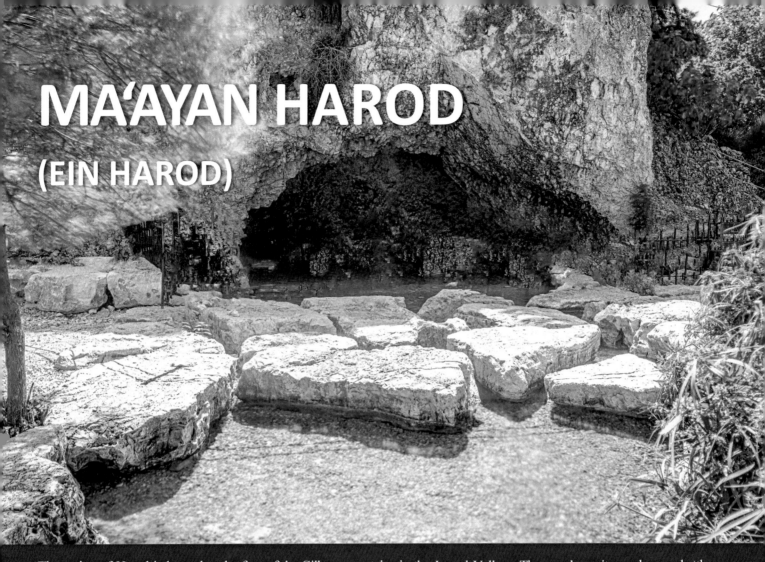

The spring of Harod is located at the foot of the Gilboa mountains in the Jezreel Valley. The area has witnessed many battles throughout history, including the famous Gideon-led battle. Gideon is one of the Hebrew judges mentioned in the Book of Judges (Chapter 7).

The Midianites were merchants and riders from the southeast, who – according to the biblical text – God allowed to be oppressed because they forgot His laws and went after the Ba'als of the Land, until they cried out and were liberated many times. On this occasion, God engaged Gideon who was doubtful whether he could rescue the Hebrews from the Midianites or not.

Ein Harod became the testing ground for such a task where Hebrews were gathered to go against the Midianites – 32.000 men showed up but 22.000 were sent home, and in the end, God chose 300 men who lapped the water like dogs. The Midianites were defeated. The main point of the story was it is through God's hand that victory is achieved and not by human effort.
King Saul and his children were also defeated by the Philistines near this place many years later. Another crucial battle took place in 1260 AD when the forces of the Mongols were moving westward like locusts but were defeated by the Mamluks' Sultan Qotuz in Ain Jalut (the Arabic name for the spring).

Above the cave spring is the house and graveyard of Yehoshua Hankin, known as the "redeemer of land". He bought the land around it and many other places from the Arab land owners of mosquito-infected swamps. Today it is a very fruitful agricultural land.
Now the site is frequently visited by many local residents for picnics and recreation.
It is administrated by the National Park Authority.

MACHPELAH
(HEBRON)

The site has been inhabited for over four thousand years and is located in the heart of the city of Hebron. This section of the book is dedicated to the enormous mausoleum where the patriarchs of the Hebrews (Abraham, Isaac and Jacob and their wives [except Rachel]) were traditionally buried. After Jerusalem, it is the second most holy place, therefore when visiting it, please respect the sanctity of the site.

The Bible tells us that Abraham bought the cave and the land around it (Genesis 23) and subsequently he was buried there as well as his son and grandson. Although the Hebrews were slaves in Egypt for many centuries, they never forgot the location of their forefathers. When the twelve spies were sent to the Promised Land, they reached Hebron (Numbers 13:22). Many Jewish exegeses believe they went to visit the cave.

According to the Israelite/Jewish history, Hebron which was given to the tribe of Judah, had a vital significance. It was from Hebron that King David started ruling over Judah for seven years and later on over all of Israel. According to the topology, the major building constructed on top of the caves seems to have been built during the 1st C BC by none other than Herod the Great. Although it remained original, structures were added to it later on.

During the Byzantine period (4th C AD), a church was added at the eastern side of the building. This section became a mosque after the Arab invasion in the 7th C AD.

In the 12th C AD during the Crusader kingdom, it reverted to being a church to eventually return to being a mosque with the re-conquest of the land by the forces of Salah ad-Din (Saladin), who ordered the construction of the minaret we see today.

According to Jewish mysticism (Zohar/Kabbalah), the Machpelah is the entrance to Gan Eden (Paradise) where anyone who entered, never returned. That was why Abraham bought the cave at such a high price. He knew Adam and Eve were also buried there, therefore souls ascended to the Garden of Eden and prayers went up to the heavenly places.

During the Mamluk period (14th-15th C AD), more transformations were made to the interior of the building which are still visible today. For instance, six cenotaphs were built indicating the tombs of Abraham and Sarah -- today shared between Muslims and Jews; Rebecca and Isaac -- in the Muslim section today; and Leah and Jacob -- in the Jewish section.

During the Muslim re-conquest of the Land after the 12th C AD, Jews and Christians were not allowed to visit the mausoleum. Instead, there was a staircase, which is no longer there, in the eastern section of the building where Jews were allowed to pray.

However, after the Six Days War of 1967, Israel took over the area, and a section of the building began to be used as a synagogue and visitors are now welcome to visit the facilities with guiding rules. Jews cannot visit the Muslim section and vice versa. Christians can visit both. However, on Fridays Christians cannot visit the mosque, and on Shabbat (Saturdays) Christians cannot visit the synagogue since these are scheduled for prayers for both groups.

Entrance is free as of the writing of this book.

MAKHTESH RAMON
(RAMON CRATER)

Makhtesh Ramon, also known as The Ramon Crater, is a beautiful and breathtaking geological formation, pretty much unique to this part of the world. There are other makhteshim (craters) in the Land but Makhtesh Ramon is the largest of them all.

Located beside the Mitzpe Ramon in the Negev, it is about 40 km in length, about 8 km in width and about 400 meter in depth. Although it resembles a crater, Makhtesh Ramon is not the result of any meteoritic impact nor a volcanic eruption. Rather, this unique phenomenon is the carving of nature i.e., karst erosion.

According to geologists, millions of years ago the entire area was covered with water since rain was very common in this area. But slowly the water started to recede northwards leaving a hump-shaped hill, which through water and wind formed the makhteshim in the Land.

There is a wide variety of flora because of the difference in the temperature between the bottom and the center of the makhtesh. It also reintroduced to nature the wild ass and Nubian ibex, which you might see during your visit or just driving by.

There is only one natural water source -- Ein Saharonim where a Khan (station for the traders) was built by the Nabateans on the incense trade route, (see Shivta, Mamshit, Avdat). There are designated areas for hiking and the best time to do it is during the fall, winter and spring, and not during summer when temperatures are quite high.

There is a visitor center managed by the Nature Reserve Authority.

MAGDALA

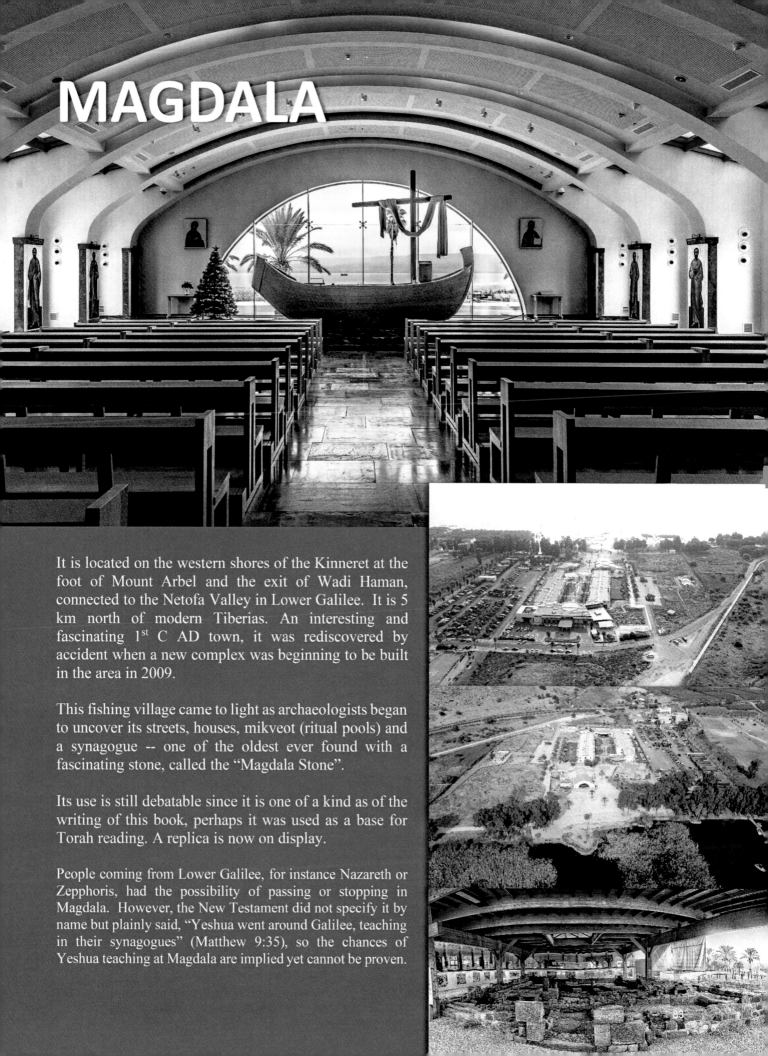

It is located on the western shores of the Kinneret at the foot of Mount Arbel and the exit of Wadi Haman, connected to the Netofa Valley in Lower Galilee. It is 5 km north of modern Tiberias. An interesting and fascinating 1st C AD town, it was rediscovered by accident when a new complex was beginning to be built in the area in 2009.

This fishing village came to light as archaeologists began to uncover its streets, houses, mikveot (ritual pools) and a synagogue -- one of the oldest ever found with a fascinating stone, called the "Magdala Stone".

Its use is still debatable since it is one of a kind as of the writing of this book, perhaps it was used as a base for Torah reading. A replica is now on display.

People coming from Lower Galilee, for instance Nazareth or Zepphoris, had the possibility of passing or stopping in Magdala. However, the New Testament did not specify it by name but plainly said, "Yeshua went around Galilee, teaching in their synagogues" (Matthew 9:35), so the chances of Yeshua teaching at Magdala are implied yet cannot be proven.

Nonetheless, Jewish historian Josephus Flavius mentioned it by its Greek name Tarichaea meaning "the places where the fish are prepared." Here the villagers had a lucrative business of dried fish.

The well-known figure of this town appearing in the pages of the New Testament was Miriam of Migdal known as Mary Magdalene, probably a businesswoman who supported the ministry of Yeshua. This was based on conjectures as hinted in Luke 8:1-3 and on the revenues yielded by the fishing industry in this town.

The villagers participated in the Jewish First Revolt of 66 AD and General Vespasian wasted no time in aborting the rebellion in the North before moving to Jerusalem.

The village was rebuilt during the last Roman period, and in the Byzantine period a monastery was built whose ruins were also uncovered.

Today there is a spiritual center dedicated to women from the Bible which is open for prayers and liturgy. They have local guides who can show you around and give you more information about the premises.

Check their website for group reservations, opening hours and entrance fees.

MAMSHIT

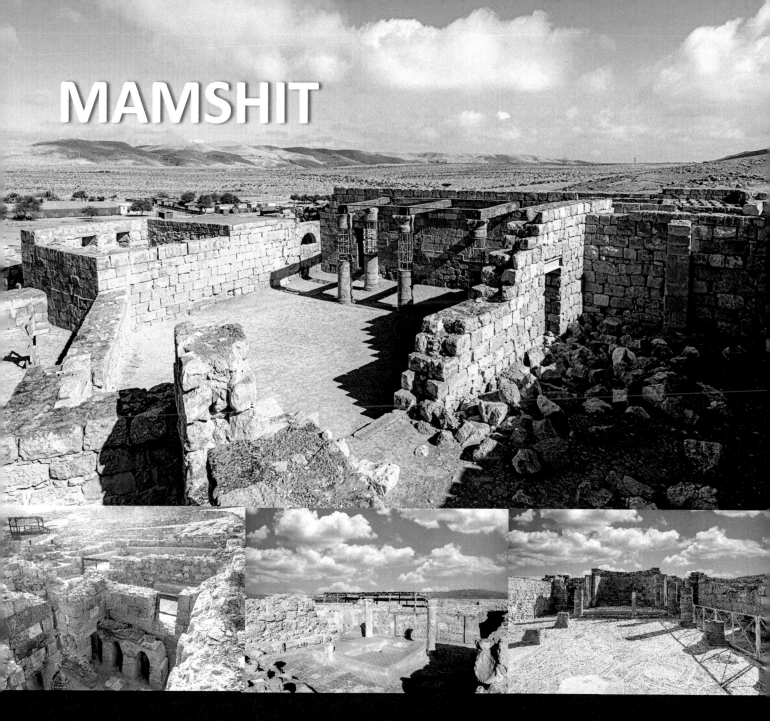

Residents of Mamshit were in the area during the second wave of Nabatean traders in the Negev around the mid-1st C BC. As their trade with the Roman Empire continued to generate revenues, their control over the Negev route became stronger.

The city was built on the second branch of the caravan route that came from Petra down to the Arava to later cross the harshness of the Negev desert before reaching the coastal plain. Therefore, control, safeguard and provision along this journey were vital.

They were smart enough to solve the biggest challenge of all -- the lack of water in the desert. They mastered the collection of flash flood water that still occurs in the desert until this very day (you can watch one of these flash floods on the author's YouTube channel: "Israel's Flash Floods in Wadi Qumran").

They successfully collected water into large cisterns intended for daily consumption, agriculture, grazing, and even for breeding the horses later to be known as Arabians. Eventually Mamshit too became part of the Roman Empire during the 2nd C AD, and written Roman sources testify that local residents were part of the Roman Militia that protected not

They were smart enough to have their own school of architecture -- the building was later on dismantled and the stones were reused in constructing one of the Churches, and the original stones can be seen in the building today.

Sadly, in the 6th C AD during the Byzantine Empire, the emperor cut the funding for Roman soldiers in that area because he concluded that it was unnecessary. This triggered the doom of Mamshit since the area was unprotected and later on the defense system of the town was destroyed and burned down.

When visiting the site, you can appreciate the large residence (the "mansion") that indicates wealth, the city walls, tower, and of course the churches which are a gem of Byzantine Nabatean architecture (some portions are still unexcavated). They were named the Nilus Church and the Eastern Church (because of their positions).

There is also the market area, a large and wide street with commerce on both sides, Nabatu House, even a bathhouse and public pool (do not miss the fresco of mythological gods Eros and Psyche on the wall).

Mamshit today is a UNESCO World Heritage Site and a National Park.

MAR SABA MONASTERY

The 3rd- 6th C AD saw an explosion of monastic life in the Judean desert -- young men in search of God and possibly of themselves, found the desert as the proper place to reach that enlightenment through prayer, fasting and work.

Their lives were inspired by the Prophet Elijah, John the Baptist and St. Anthony of Egypt, the father of monastic life.

On the other hand, the father of the Judean monastic life was St. Chariton the Confessor 3rd C AD.

Much can be said about how these men began their journeys as hermits living in caves or Laura, meeting only once a week in the Judean desert and near the Dead Sea area, to later organize themselves in what is known as coenobium or monastery with regulations to follow.

During this time period dozens of monasteries and churches were built across the Judean desert but this book will only cover two of them: Mar Saba and St. George (see St. George of Koziba Monastery).

Mar Saba Monastery was established by St. Sabas or Mar Sabas from Cappadocia, who came to Jerusalem at age 18 and never returned home. For almost half a century, he led the Laura that is today Mar Saba, whose cave is still there. Sabas helped established other monasteries in the region as the desert flourished during this time period.

He died at age 93 and was buried where the monastery bearing his name is located today.

His bones were taken to Venice by the Crusaders during the Crusader kingdom but were returned to the monastery in 1965. Today these are on display inside the main church. An aedicula is in the court yard where he was originally buried. They have strict rules for women visiting the premises -- they are only allowed to go to the women's tower and look over the monastery from the outside.

Pictures are not allowed inside unless one gains special permission from the Greek Patriarch or finds grace from the monk who oversees the visit – this author was only allowed to take two. The monastery has gone through different phases of riots, destruction and expansion. It was built 10 km east of Bethlehem, hanging from the cliff of the Kidron Valley, starting from Jerusalem and ending by the Dead Sea.

It has an overwhelming view and tranquility and the journey down is certainly an adventure with very steep roads. The monastery is closed to the public on Wednesdays and Fridays. These are the days the monks are praying and fasting, but it is open the rest of the week at 09:00.

MASADA

However, it was not just a place of refuge but a palace as well with all the luxury of that time period. Palaces, store rooms, cisterns, pools, Roman baths, stucco and fresco decoration, you name it they had it -- Herod did not neglect to equip it with anything but the best.

Construction basically took place immediately when Herod began ruling in 37 BC and was finished by 31 BC. After his death in 4 BC, Roman guards were assigned to protect the area, which was later taken by the Sicarii led by Eleazar Ben Yair, and 960 men including women and children sought refuge on top of the mountain after the fall of Jerusalem in 70 AD.

However, the Romans did not tolerate this group of rebels hiding on top of a rock for more than three years. Roman soldiers brought down those men, sending a message through the Roman Empire that Rome would not tolerate this type of insurrection.

The question that many historians ask is: "How can a man, in this case Josephus Flavius, who was not an eye witness, give so many details of the account, especially of Eliezer Ben Yair? Here is how archaeology and written history differ from each other.

According to Flavius, Ben Yair convinced the men to kill their wives and children then kill each other instead of being captured and made slaves or simply being killed (Josephus Flavius, The War of the Jews, VII). According to Flavius only one woman and four children survived since they were hidden in one of the water cisterns. Did she tell the story to Flavius when she got to Rome? We do not know!

MAZOR
MAUSOLEUM

MEGIDDO
(TEL MEGGIDO)

The city of kings. Located in one of the most strategic areas of the land in the ancient world, protecting the entrance of the Jezreel Valley that connected The Way of the Sea (Via Maris) to Mesopotamia and the kingdoms of Mittani. Its relevance and strategic location made it to the historical records of the temple in Karnak, Egypt. Pharaoh Thutmose III in the 15th C BC battled the king of Megiddo and took the area by surprise after he decided to rebel, assuming the Mittani would back him up. It was the first recorded battle in the history of the Jezreel Valley, where he conquered and plundered the city.

Every empire that controlled this land secured the passage to this valley. It is no wonder that Protestant Christians named the area the Valley of Armageddon because of the many battles fought on its soil. Megiddo's early habitation dates from the Neolithic period (7th and 6th millennia) and the Chalcolithic period (5th and 4th Millennia BC). When King David conquered the hill, we see today it had twenty different layers of civilization. Joshua and the Judges were unable to conquer it (Joshua 17:11-13; Judges 1:27).

The Bible tells us that Solomon rebuilt Megiddo as he did with Hazor and Gezer (1 Kings 19:15). Today with much careful examination of the sites, scholars have concluded that the golden Israelite period of Megiddo took place during the 9th and 8th C BC under the reign of Ahab and Jeroboam II when massive gates, palaces, stables and an incredible hydro-engineering project were completed using rural yet sophisticated tools. Megiddo was taken in 732 BC by Tiglath-Pileser III and subsequently the Persians left behind a rich legacy

It was rediscovered over two millenniums later in the 19th C AD. A new story of Megiddo began again when explorers and archaeologists started uncovering its past, attracting millions of visitors through the decades of becoming a National Park and a UNESCO World Heritage site. When visiting, expect to see the Late Bronze Age Canaanite Gate which was more of a ceremonial gate leading to the palace area than a protective gate. It was destroyed by the time the Israelites took over the place and rebuilt it one century later.

When entering the site, you will see on the left an Israelite staircase leading to a reservoir. It is not clear where the water came from. On top there are remnants of stables located on the north and south of the site, either built by Ahab in the 9th C BC or Jeroboam II in 8th C BC, as well as the corresponding palaces and the incredible Israelite water system supplying the city especially when under siege. The massive temple area dates from the fourth millennium BC and the same site has been used century after century without losing its sanctity. The Assyrian palace and quarters. Its granary was built either at the end of the Israelite period or during the Assyrian period. Last but not least, the Persian left behind

MIGDAL AFEK CASTLE (MIRABEL)

The site is also known as Migdal Tzedek (the Tower of Righteousness in Hebrew), located in a very strategic area in the ancient period. Ethnographic studies of the areas show pottery that was associated with what is known as the Iron Age II (late Israelite period) and the Roman period. The area overlooks the narrow passage of the ancient highway known during the Roman and later periods as the Via Maris (Way of the Sea).

It was an extension to Antipatris (see Aphek) which together with Migdal Tzedek, participated in the Great Revolt that led to the final destruction of Jerusalem in 70 AD. During the late Roman and Byzantine periods, the area was rebuilt as evidenced by traces of re-used stones (that can even be used as lintels) with Greek inscriptions taken from a church here that was presumably destroyed in the 7th C AD. It was dedicated to St. Cyriacus who the legend says was a rich man who gave his wealth to the poor. As Yeshua told the rich man in the Bible to give his wealth to the poor and follow Him, so did Cyriacus, who also attended to the poor and later became a martyr during the persecution under Emperor Diocletian in 303 AD.

Therefore, in his honor, a monastery was located on this site. The Crusaders as well as previous periods saw how strategic the location was, hence the Mirabel was built by a noble family (Ibelin Family) who had vast possessions throughout the Holy Land. They remained in the Land up to the end of the 13th C AD. After the fierce and bloody Battle of Hattin in 1187 AD when the Crusaders were defeated, Mirabel was taken by the Ayyubids and used until 1191 AD to prevent the Crusaders from regaining control in upcoming crusades. It was rebuilt by the Mamluks in the 13th C AD and eventually abandoned. Migdal Tzedek was rebuilt during the 19th C AD (which forms most of the structure we see today) by a predominant Bedouin Al-Sadik from Samaria, to collect taxes from local villagers but the Turks were not so pleased about this, so he was exiled from Palestine.
Today Migdal Tzedek is a National Park and as of the writing of this book admission is free.

MONFORT
CASTLE

It is located in the upper-west of Galilee. An excellent vantage point in Goren Park gives a magnificent view of the fortress-castle. Goren Park is open to the public free of charge. It is a beautiful area for recreation for family or groups and even as a campsite where everyone can experience the freedom of enjoying nature. It is a stunning green area which makes you forget you are actually in an area where 60% of the terrain is a desert. You can enjoy the Israeli oak (Quercus calliprinos) which is very common in the Mediterranean woodlands, the Palestine pistachio, the spiny hawthorn, and carob trees, among others. Designated hiking areas are well-marked (please follow the trail), so enjoy and protect the scenery and the flora and fauna of the park.

The castle, which is one of the most impressive castles found in the country, was built during the Crusader kingdom in the 12th-13th C AD. Previously a farm was established by a noble Crusader family from nearby villages. The last one to occupy the fortress was the Teutonic order (German Knights). It is incredible to see trees growing between its walls even after its destruction by the Mamluks at the end of the same century. From the outstanding vantage point visitors can hike all the way to the castle, just follow the marked lines and do so only in designated areas. Goren Park and Montfort Castle are under the protection of the Nature Reserve Authority. As of the writing of this book, there is no admission fee for the park. Refer to their website for further information.

MOUNT CARMEL
(MUKHRAKA)

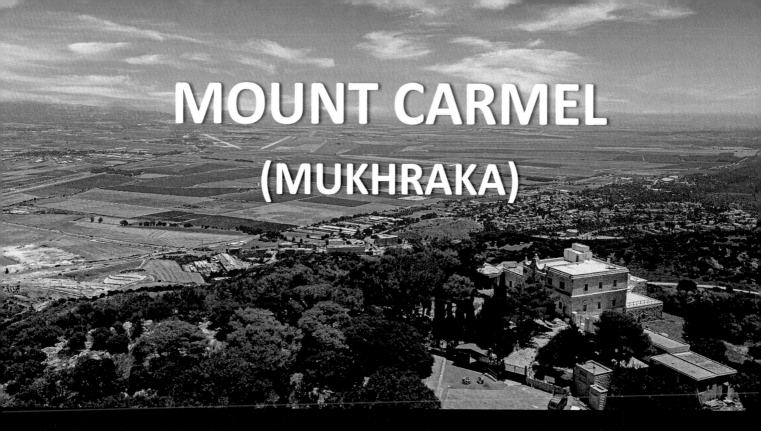

It is a mountain range 39 km long and 8 km wide with an elevation of 525 meters above sea level. Unlike other mountain ranges in the country, Carmel runs northwest to southeast. It marked the boundaries between Israelite tribes: Asher, Zebulon, Issachar and the half-tribe of Manasseh, however the mountain itself was given to Asher (Joshua 19:26).

Thutmose III in his campaign in the Land of Retjenu called it "The Holy Head".
Mount Carmel has been blessed with the dew of the morning because of its proximity to the Mediterranean Sea, making the area green all year round.

One of the most remarkable biblical events that took place in Mount Carmel was Elijah's confrontation with the prophets of Baal and Ashera (1 Kings 18). The people at this time (9th C BC) became syncretistic -- worshipped the God of Israel and at the same time continuing the Canaanite worship.

The worship of Baal and Ashera was common even before the coming of the Hebrews into the Land, and although the Hebrew religion claimed the existence of one true God, it took centuries and periods of exile from their Land until they finally adopted a monotheistic religion. However, before that, one of their major prophets, Elijah from Tishbe (Transjordan), not only confronted the people to make up their minds as to who was the true God, but he challenged King Ahab too at the risk of losing his own life.

Carmel was not chosen randomly but Elijah, who knew the worship of Baal on the mountain, challenged them in their own territory. And although Jerusalem was supposed to be the only place to offer sacrifice to the God of the Israelites, He honored his prophet and burned the entire offering without anyone lighting any fire on it.

Elijah's message is still very significant today. Some cultures might be bowing down to images carved by human hands or to trivial things like money, family, earthly possession, etc., which might be taking the place of God. God is a jealous God and He will not share His glory with anyone or anything. If the God of Abraham is God, then worship Him alone.

This message and the symbol of Elijah inspired Christians during the Crusader period 12th C AD, who came to this area and started to live as hermits in caves until they organized themselves in a community, giving birth to the Carmelite Order, named after the mountain.

After the fall of the Crusader kingdom in the 12th -13th C AD, the Carmelites were expelled by the returning Muslim forces, then went back to Europe where they flourished throughout the continent for centuries.

Eventually they returned to their place of origin in the 17th C but they were not allowed to rebuild right away. The present monastery and the church of Elijah were built in the mid to end of the 19th C AD.

Be sure not to miss an incredible viewpoint on top of the shop which overlooks the Jezreel Valley and on clear days you can see Lower Galilee, Gilboa Mountains and even the Mediterranean Sea.

MOUNT GERIZIM

Throughout the millennia this mountain has been holy and of historical of importance for Jews, Samaritans and even Christians. It is also known as the Mount of the Blessing where blessings were read by Joshua, the son of Nun, while curses were read in Mount Ebal (Deuteronomy 11:29, 27:1-13; Joshua 8:33-35). The nearby area was once the capital of the Kingdom of Israel until 732 BC when the Northern Kingdom was taken by the Assyrians. Located here today is the modern Palestinian city of Nablus.

There is a misconception and sensational urban legend of the so-called "ten lost Tribes of Israel". Today we know historically, biblically, and archaeologically that not everyone from the northern kingdom was exiled except the elite and royal family. The poor and the common people were left behind to keep working the land. The Samaritans originated during this period as new people were brought from other parts of the Assyrian Empire and merged with the remaining local population of the northern tribes.

This new breed of people eventually adopted the beliefs of those who were left behind and re-interpreted their scriptures (the five books of Moses). For instance, Jerusalem was not the place of worship for the God of Abraham but rather in Mount Gerizim. Also, the land of Moriah where Abraham went to offer Isaac was on Mount Gerizim.

Animosity grew between the local Samaritans and returnees from exile. They later rebuilt the land under Zerubbabel, Ezra, and Nehemiah (Ezra 4:1-5). The rift between these two groups of people continued through history and we see this reflected in the gospel according to John 4 (see Jacob's Well).

Since the Jews returning from exile did not allow the Samaritans to participate in rebuilding the Temple in Jerusalem, the latter built their own on Mount Gerizim and the area around the temple flourished during the Hellenistic period (4th-1st C BC).
However, both their temple and town were destroyed during the Hasmonean's expansion of their kingdom and forced proselytization led by the Hasmonean King John Hyrcanus I 112th -111th BC (Josephus Ant, 13 10:3).

This all changed with the coming of Pompey in 63 BC who annexed the entire area to the Roman Empire. The Samaritans rebuilt their city with the exception of their temple, though a temple to Zeus was built nearby during the 2nd C AD.

The Samaritans continued flourishing all the way to the Byzantine era and clashed with the new Christian Roman Empire. Emperor Zeno built a church in 484 AD that led to a confrontation with the Byzantine rulers in the 6th C AD.

Emperor Justinian did not just reinforce the established church whose ruins can still be seen today, but almost exterminated them to a point from which they have hardly recovered until this very day, having less than one thousand Samaritans on the planet. The church area continued to be used during the early Islamic invasion as well the Crusader period.

Today you can visit the mountain with a breathtaking view of the modern city of Nablus and the archaeological remains of the Byzantine church dedicated to Mary, the mother of Yeshua.
Check with the National Park Authority for opening hours and entrance fees.
On top of the mountain, there is a small Samaritan Museum where their high priest or one of their staff members can talk to visitors or tourists based on pre-approved arrangements.

MOUNT OF BEATITUDES

Matthew 5 and Luke 6 are very well-known passages among many Christians who call it the Sermon on the Mount.

We need to pay attention for a moment as to how Matthew tried to present the One greater than Moses. For instance, Moses went up to Mount Sinai, and Yeshua goes up into a mountain and gives an interpretation of the Torah (Pentateuch) on how to use these instructions for our daily lives.

Note that He sat down, something which is strange in our culture today but very normal for the time -- a very typical Jewish custom of sitting down when a teacher was instructing.

Matthew, who was very well acquainted with the area, gave no specific location for this mountain, except that he went up to it. However, early Jewish believers from Capernaum most likely knew where it was and could have passed on that information orally to the next generations.

By the 4th C AD, the pilgrim Egeria spoke of a cave near Tabgha upon which the Lord ascended after teaching the Beatitudes. She could only have heard this from local believers of Yeshua in the area.

By the end of the same century, a church was built to commemorate this event but it was sadly destroyed in the 7th C AD and was never rebuilt.

MOUNT TABOR

Matthew 17:1-8 tells us that Yeshua took His closest disciples -- Peter, John and Jacob (James) --with Him into a high mountain. Once again for Matthew, the exact location of the mountain was irrelevant, but the center of the story is the event of the Transfiguration.

We read how out of "nowhere" two predominant biblical characters showed up talking to Yeshua – Moses and Elijah, representing the messianic kingdom. The disciples had no idea what all this meant, hence Peter jumped in and suggested making three tabernacles. The question is, how did Peter know who these men were? Did he overhear the conversation introducing them to Yeshua? We do not know; the text simply does not tell us.

Similarly, at the beginning of Yeshua's ministry while He was being baptized by John, a voice was heard from heavens: This is my son (Psalm 2:7 "You are my son…") in whom I am well pleased (Isaiah 42:1 "Behold my servant, whom I uphold, my chosen, in whom my soul delights…") Listen to him (Deuteronomy 18: 15 The LORD your God will raise up for you a prophet like me from among you, from your fellow Israelites. You must listen to Him).

After such a manifestation, they were commanded not to tell anyone until after the resurrection.

By the 4th C AD Christians coming on pilgrimages to what they would later call the Holy Land, also wanted to know where this event took place. Since Matthew did not give any exact location, several suggestions were proposed: Eusebius was not sure if it was Mount Hermon or Mount Tabor, the pilgrim from Bordeaux pointed to the Mount of Olives. However, in 348 AD Cyril of Jerusalem decided it was Mount Tabor, which later was firmly backed up by the church father Jerome.

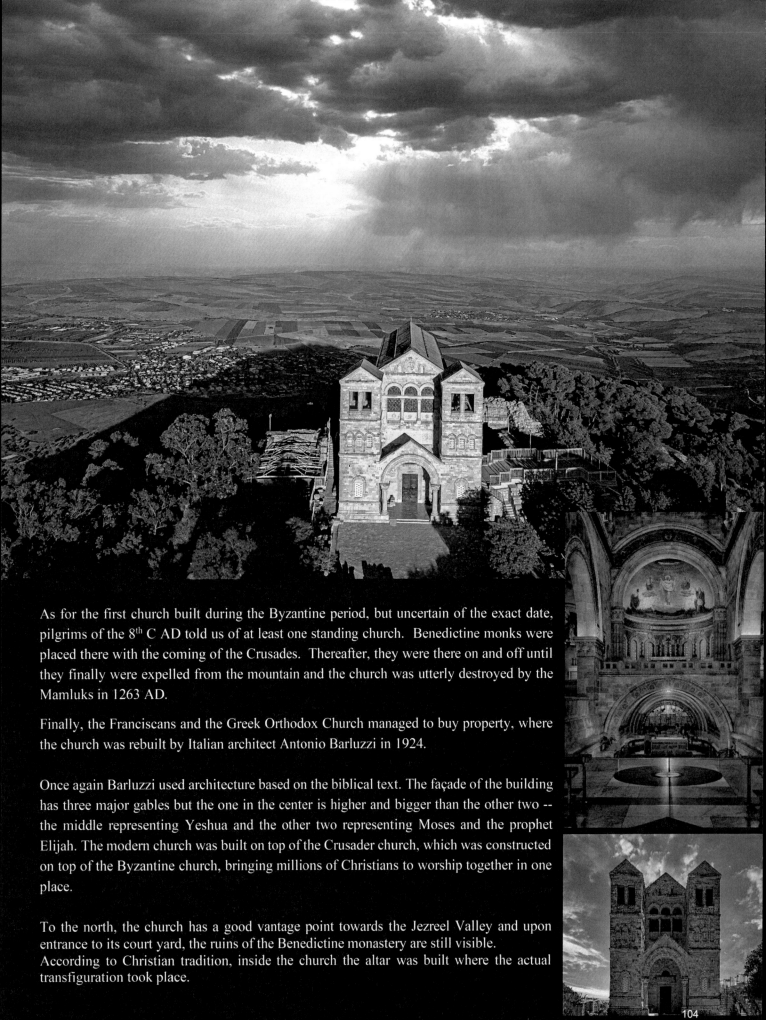

As for the first church built during the Byzantine period, but uncertain of the exact date, pilgrims of the 8th C AD told us of at least one standing church. Benedictine monks were placed there with the coming of the Crusades. Thereafter, they were there on and off until they finally were expelled from the mountain and the church was utterly destroyed by the Mamluks in 1263 AD.

Finally, the Franciscans and the Greek Orthodox Church managed to buy property, where the church was rebuilt by Italian architect Antonio Barluzzi in 1924.

Once again Barluzzi used architecture based on the biblical text. The façade of the building has three major gables but the one in the center is higher and bigger than the other two -- the middle representing Yeshua and the other two representing Moses and the prophet Elijah. The modern church was built on top of the Crusader church, which was constructed on top of the Byzantine church, bringing millions of Christians to worship together in one place.

To the north, the church has a good vantage point towards the Jezreel Valley and upon entrance to its court yard, the ruins of the Benedictine monastery are still visible.
According to Christian tradition, inside the church the altar was built where the actual transfiguration took place.

NAHAL TANINIM

Literally meaning 'Crocodile River', this nature reserve covers the river from its source Ramot Menashe until it empties into the Mediterranean Sea. It marks the southern limit to the Carmel coastal plain. During the late Roman period, Nahal Taninim provided water to Caesarea Maritima. At its zenith, dams and aqueducts were built to provide additional water to the city where the demand was high.

Was the name a misnomer or did crocodiles actually live here or in the Land of the Messiah as a whole? As a matter of fact, yes, they actually did, from prehistoric times until the end of the 19th C AD. The area was a swamp until it was finally drained at the beginning of the 20th C AD due to the infestation of mosquitos transmitting malaria. During the Roman period, there was even a town nearby called Krokodilopolis named after the crocodiles living in the swamps. Using the power of the dam, the inhabitants of the area built six flour mills powered by water during the Byzantine period.

While taking a pleasant walk in the Nature Reserve, visitors can see the burial caves, the Nahal Taninim dam, low-level aqueduct, low-aqueduct, and even a stone quarry all from the late Roman period.

NAZARETH

CAN ANY GOOD THING COME OUT OF NAZARETH?

These were the words of Nathanael when he heard from Philip that they had found the one Moses wrote about in the Torah and foretold by the Prophets -- Yeshua the son of Joseph (John 1:44-45).

With such a doubtful but sincere question, one might wonder what brought Nazareth such a bad reputation? Nazareth in the 1st C AD was a very small town which, according to the ethnography studies done by archaeologists, had a few hundred people.

Its insignificance caused Jewish Roman historian Josephus Flavius to not even mention and ignore it despite its proximity to Zippori, the capital of Galilee. This triggered the curiosity of Bible scholars for the statement quoted in the gospel of John.

After Joseph was warned by an angel and used his common sense, they returned from Egypt and decided to settle in Nazareth where perhaps they had some close relatives (Matthew 2:20-23).

Yeshua began his ministry in His hometown Nazareth but He was rejected by His peers and neighbors who had seen Him growing up, and found it ridiculous and inconceivable that the Son of the craftsman Joseph would be the Messiah and they even thought of killing Him. But He walked through them and using His common sense, moved to Capernaum (Matthew 4:14-31).

As Christians began going on pilgrimages to what they would later call the Holy Land, one of the well-known pilgrims was a woman named Egeria who came between 381 and 384 AD. She mentioned that the adoration grotto (cave) which tradition claimed as the house of Mary was also the place of the annunciation of the Archangel Gabriel. Additionally, the latter told Mary in this place that she would become the bearer of the Messiah and gave her a promise that is yet to be fulfilled since David's kingdom has yet to be restored…

"…The Lord God will give him the throne of his father David, and he will reign over Jacob's descendants forever; his kingdom will never end." - Luke 1:32-33.

Since Egeria made no mention of a church, it is assumed that it was built sometime in the 5th C AD. But it was destroyed in the 7th C AD and rebuilt during the Crusader period at the beginning of the 12th C AD. It was eventually destroyed again in the 13th C AD by the Mamluks. After the Franciscans were expelled from the Land, they returned in the 17th C AD and purchased the land where the church lay in ruins, but they were not allowed to rebuild until the 18th C AD.

Due to the number of visitors, the modest church building was demolished in order to build a basilica making it the largest in the Middle East as of the writing of this book. The new church building has traces of the previous church buildings, making the grotto (cave) from the 1st C AD the center of worship.

However, the Eastern Church pointed a few hundred meters away from the Latin Church to a square known as Fontana di Maria (Mary's Well) where the tradition of the Annunciation by the Archangel Gabriel took place. And the church named after the Archangel Gabriel was built in the 18th C AD on the ruins of the Crusader church which was originally constructed during the Byzantine period and was destroyed in the 13th C AD.

In the town market there is a Greek Catholic church known as the Synagogue Church although the church building was erected in the Middle Ages.

NIMROD FORTRES

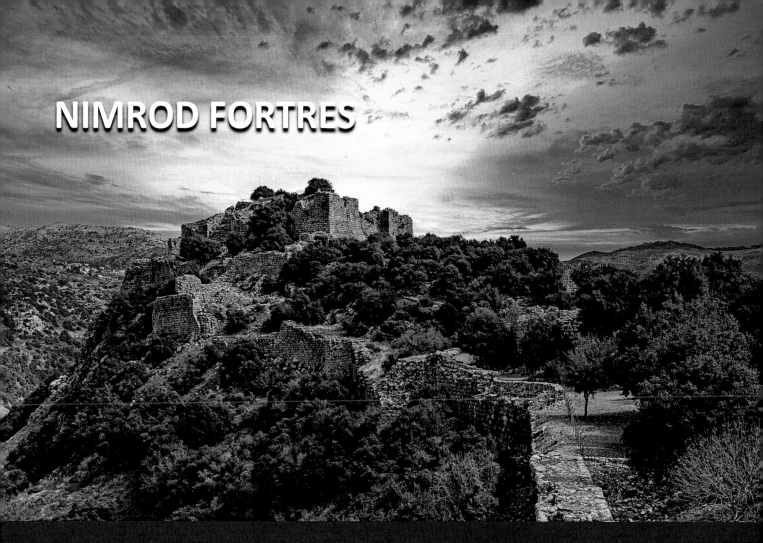

Also known in Arabic as Qal'at Subayba (the Cliff Fortress). According to Arabic legend, the strong hunter Nimrod, king of Shinar and great-grandson of Noah, was punished by Allah in this place by putting a mosquito inside his head that drove him crazy. Another legend says that Nimrod built his castle here and from it, he extended his long arm to draw water from the Banias below the mountain.

Although the Crusaders lost control of most of the 1st Crusader kingdom after their humiliating defeat in the Horns of Hattin in 1187 AD near the Kinneret, they managed to gain control of the coastal plain.

The Ayyubids systematically destroyed the entire Crusader strongholds preventing them from keeping hold of the Land. Subsequently the Crusaders attempted several times to reconquer the Land but they failed.

The area of Banias was under the control of the men of Salah ad-Din (Saladin). Rivalry between the governors of Egypt (Sultan Al-Malik Al-Kamal) and Damascus (Al-Mou'azzam Issa), who happened to be brothers, led to the building of the fortress in 1227 AD.

This was because Al-Mou'azzam feared the return of the Crusaders, especially when his brother made an alliance with Frederick II. The fortress was later completed in 1230 AD.

Nonetheless, the Crusaders did not give up and tried again to reconquer the area but failed terribly in 1253 AD. A few years later, the Mongol invasion from central Asia brought about the destruction of the fortress, though they were stopped near Mount Gilboa (see Ein Harod).

The Mamluks rebuilt the fortress after their triumph over the Mongols which was considered one of the most important battles in history. With the final expulsion of the Crusaders from the whole land in 1291 AD, the importance of the fortress diminished in the 15th C AD after it served as a prison for rebels, and was eventually abandoned, to be reused by local shepherds seeking temporary refuge.

Today it is run by the National Park Authority.

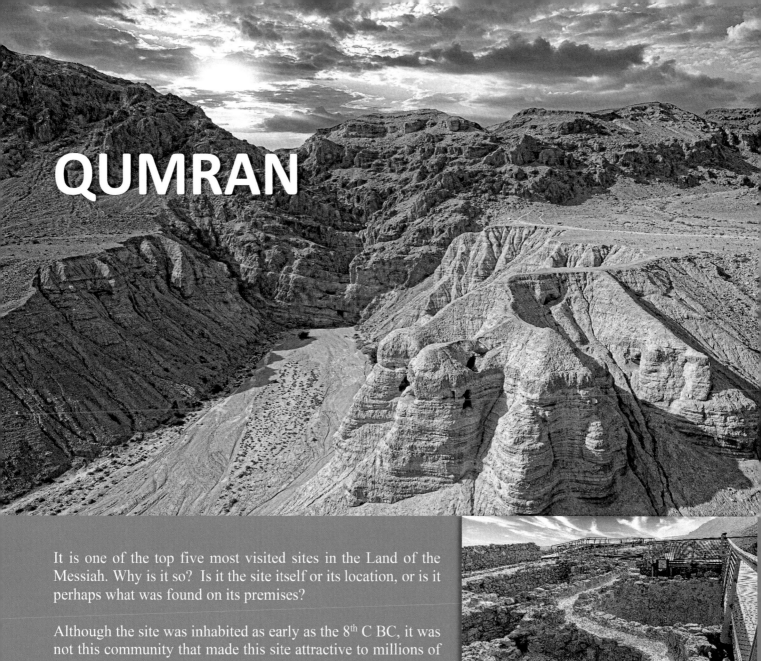

QUMRAN

It is one of the top five most visited sites in the Land of the Messiah. Why is it so? Is it the site itself or its location, or is it perhaps what was found on its premises?

Although the site was inhabited as early as the 8th C BC, it was not this community that made this site attractive to millions of visitors over the last decades. Rather, it was the type of community in the 2nd C BC, known to some as the Essenes or the Qumran community, that made visitors want to come.

The details of who they were and what they did are beyond the scope of this book. On its premises were found the number one discovery of the 20th C, and since then tons of research materials and books have been written about these people living in this area. According to the consensus of the scholars, this community wrote the Dead Sea Scrolls.

The community arrived in the area at the end of the 2nd C BC due in part to the corruption of the priesthood and kingship in Jerusalem. They too were expecting God's intervention in human history by sending two Messiahs -- Messiah Ben Yoseph, a meek and humble Messiah, and Messiah Ben David, a warrior and liberator.

This community radically was obsessed with the study of the scriptures, daily purification, bathing and prayer.
In 31 BC a major earthquake forced the community to leave; however, they came back during Archelaus rule at the end of the 1st C BC.

During the Great Revolt in 66-73 AD, the Roman forces took over the site (68 AD) and dispersed the community. Some fled to Jerusalem, others to Masada. Both encountered their final fate.
There is no historical, archaeological or biblical evidence that John the Baptist was part of this community despite its proximity to the Jordan River where he baptized.

Roman soldiers were left on the site right after the Second Revolt in 132-135 AD. Eventually the site was abandoned and forgotten until accidentally, a local Bedouin found seven scrolls hidden in clay jars and the race began between scholars and Bedouins in search of more scrolls.
Father R. de Vaux and a team of French archaeologists began excavating the site and its surrounding area and additional scrolls were found. Due to low humidity, those hidden in jars were preserved for almost two millenniums like books from the TeNaCh (O.T.) along with Apocryphal writings and scrolls about themselves and their daily practices.

Ever since their discovery, the study of the scrolls has shed much light on the world of the late Second Temple period.
Today some of the scrolls are on display at the Shrine of the Book in the Israel Museum in Jerusalem.
Today the site is managed by the National Park Authority.

RAMLA

The city of Ramla was built in the 8th C AD. The first city in the Land of the Messiah to be founded by Muslims during the Umayyad Empire, it has been re-occupied thereafter by different powers that swept through this land, among them: Abbasid, Fatimids, Seljuqs, Crusaders, Ayyubids, Mamluks, Ottomans, and today Israel.

The city was strategically built on the ancient Via Maris controlling the passageway between south and north. It has several attractions now for visitors such as the Compound of the (Square) White Tower.

Much of the famous White Mosque was built in the 8th C AD and rebuilt during the Ayyubids and Mamluks time.

The most complete structure is the White Tower completed in 1318 AD by Sultan Muhammad Ibn Khaldun.

However, there is a debate between scholars as to the purpose of the tower. Some have suggested that it served as a watch tower overlooking the coastal plain, Judean Mountains and Samaria. Others have suggested that it was just a minaret for the muezzin to call the faithful Muslims to come and pray five times a day.

Another attraction the city offers is the well-preserved Pool of the Arches, one of the few existing examples of Abbasid architecture in the region in 789 AD.

The site presents a rare example of the method of building by early Muslim architecture. The pool was fed by a main aqueduct from nearby Gezer to the reservoir under the White Tower's structure.

Today it serves as entertainment for families who come to row between the pointed arches where three rows of columns were built from stone.

Every row has five columns and the roof rests on pointed arches, even the hatches are visible, perhaps serving previous generations to draw water from the pool.

Other attractions in Ramla are: Ramla Museum, Ramla Market, the Great Mosque, the Greek Orthodox Monastery of St. Georgios, the Franciscan Church of St. Nicodemus and Joseph of Arimathea, the Karaite Judaism center, among others.

ROSH HANIKRA

This is a magnificent natural attraction located on the northwestern border of Israel and Lebanon where the sea meets the cliff. Beautiful grottoes (caves) were formed through the ages as the waves hit the cliff made of chalk rock.

There was an ancient legend of a young girl from near the city of Akko whose father arranged for her to marry a rich but old man from Lebanon. One day the young girl with her father and family journeyed to Tzur in Lebanon where the ceremony was to take place. When they were passing Rosh Hanikra, the girl jumped off her horse into the stormy sea and was never seen again. That is why when entering the mysterious grotto, if you pay close attention, you may hear her singing a melancholy song.

Whether the story is true or not, we simply do not know, but that does not take away the mysterious and romantic aspects of the site.

During the British Mandate, South African soldiers blasted the caves to make way for the Lebanon-Haifa railway leaving a section of the rail visible today. The grotto is reached by a very steep cable car with a gradient of 60% and believed to be one of the steepest cable cars in the world. The site can be visited all year round.

SAINT PETER PRIMACY

The events we read about in John 21 are after the resurrection. Yeshua's disciples had returned to their old profession (some were fishermen) in Galilee.

As was their custom some of them went fishing all night without catching anything. Exhausted and perhaps disappointed, they met Yeshua early in the morning on the shore, not recognizing Him until He instructed them to throw their nets to the right side.

However, the central point of John 21 was not the catching of the fish, but rather restoring Peter to his former calling -- to be a fisher of men. After Peter repented for denying Yeshua three times, Yeshua reassured him of his calling to attend to, take care of and feed His flock.

Then He asked Peter three times if he loved Him which was for Peter's sake and not Yeshua's. Peter had publicly denied knowing Him three times, so Yeshua needed to restore him publicly too so that people would not doubt the other disciples, and to remind Peter not to worry about others but to follow Yeshua.

For this very reason, early Christians looked for this site in order to remember and venerate these holy places.

Egeria who came between 381 and 384 AD mentioned the place as the Mensa Christi (Christ's Table) where the tradition she heard from the local believers was where Yeshua served breakfast to His disciples. She did not make any mention of the church building which leads us to believe that it was built later on.

Somehow the church lasted longer than the others around the lake since it was mentioned in the 9th C AD, as well as the six heart-shaped stones named as the twelve thrones, although we do not know their practical use. Inevitably the church was destroyed in 1263 AD.

The present chapel was built upon the ruins of the early church constructed in 1933 under the custodian of the Franciscans. It was built on the shore of the Kinneret giving direct access to its water where you can dip your feet and collect some small pebbles. Swimming is not allowed.

SEA
OF GALILEE

Located in the Syrian African Rift, southeast of Galilee and the Golan Heights to the east. It is about 53 km in circumference, 21 km from north to south, 13 km from east to west with a maximum depth of approximately 44 meters. The area was inhabited as early as the Netufian culture (about 12000-9500 BC) when a village from this time period was found in Ein Gev.

This body of water has been known by many names through its history depending on the inhabitants around its shorelines: Kinneret Lake, Sea of Galilee, and Sea of Kinneret, which according to the consensus among scholars was connected to the ancient city from the late Bronze Age and Iron Age as Kinneret (Tel-Oreimeh).

It has been suggested that the lake is named after the city and not the other way around. It is also known as Lake of Gennesaret, Sea of Ginosar, Sea of Tiberias, Lake Tiberias, etc. The area of the sea is an extension of the Via Maris connecting Egypt to Damascus and Mesopotamia that led the ancient powers who had control over the surrounding areas to develop cities and towns around its premises.

Tourism has become an important part of the lake due to its connection to Yeshua and biblical references to His ministry around the lake such as: the drowning of the pigs (Mark 5:1-20), Yeshua frequently crossed the area (Matthew 8:23; Mark 8:10), the miracle of the calming of the waters (Matthew 8:23-27), Yeshua walked on the water (Matthew 14:22-33), miracle of the enormous catch (Luke 5:1-11), miracle of Peter's fish (Matthew 17:24-27), Yeshua restored Peter (John 21), and others. Not to mention all the holy places around the lake: Capernaum, Magdala, Tabgha (the feeding

Before the State of Israel developed other alternatives for providing water to its inhabitants through desalination and recycling, the lake provided most of the drinkable water. As of the writing of this book, about 15% of its water is used for different forms of daily consumption.

Some of the discoveries from the Sea of Galilee in the last few decades were Magdala (see Magdala) and the so-called "Jesus' Boat" which is actually an ancient fishing boat from the 1st C AD. Towards the end of the Ottoman Empire in 1917, the areas around the shores of the lake saw agricultural development and a boom in farming until this very day with the establishment of communal farming villages known as Kibbutz (1909).

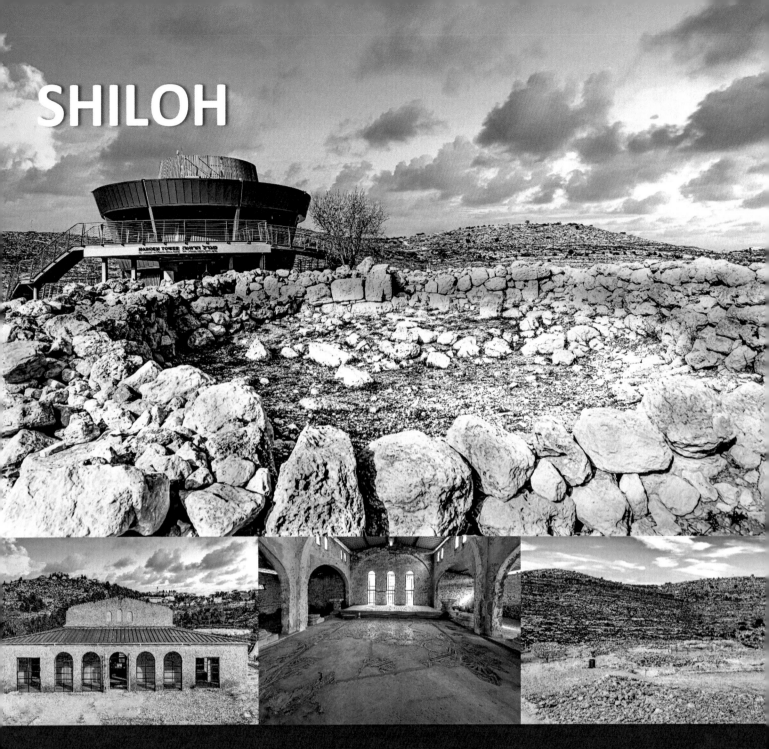

SHILOH

Before the advent of the Israelites, Shiloh was already a walled city from the Middle Bronze Age (18th-16th C BC) with a well-established center of worship. This was determined by the cultic material culture found there. The hill country of the half tribe of Manasseh and Ephraim began to be inhabited during the 13th-12th C BC, making Shiloh the spiritual capital of the tribes, since the Ark of the Covenant rested there for about four centuries.

Some of the tribes were assigned the portion of their land at Shiloh (Joshua 18:1-19:51); this included the Levitical cities (Joshua 21:1-2). Due to the presence in Shiloh of the Ark of the Covenant that represented the presence of God, the children of Israel began to go on pilgrimages to its site (Judges 21:19). Shiloh was the home of Eli the priest and mentor of Samuel the prophet, whose mother Hannah prayed for a child (1 Samuel 1:1-19). After the fierce battle against the Philistines at Ebenezer when they began penetrating through the hills area, the Ark of the Covenant was taken and brought to Ashdod (1 Samuel 5:1).

Shiloh was destroyed in the 11th C BC presumably right after the battle of Ebenezer. It lay in ruins for over a century, was rebuilt by the Northern Kingdom sometime later in the 7th C BC to eventually fall again between 722 and 712 BC. The kings of Assyria Shalmaneser and Sargon II took into captivity the royal family, the elite, and a high official leaving behind the poor to continue working on the Land (2 Kings 17:5-6).

Shiloh was inhabited again during the Roman and Byzantine periods. Church buildings were built during the Byzantine period and one of its mosaics helped identify the site with the biblical Shiloh that earlier Christians were also venerating.

Many churches in the 7th C AD were systematically destroyed by the Persian invasion and many of them were never rebuilt. During the Ottoman period in the southern area of ancient Shiloh, a mosque was built and named

SHIVTA

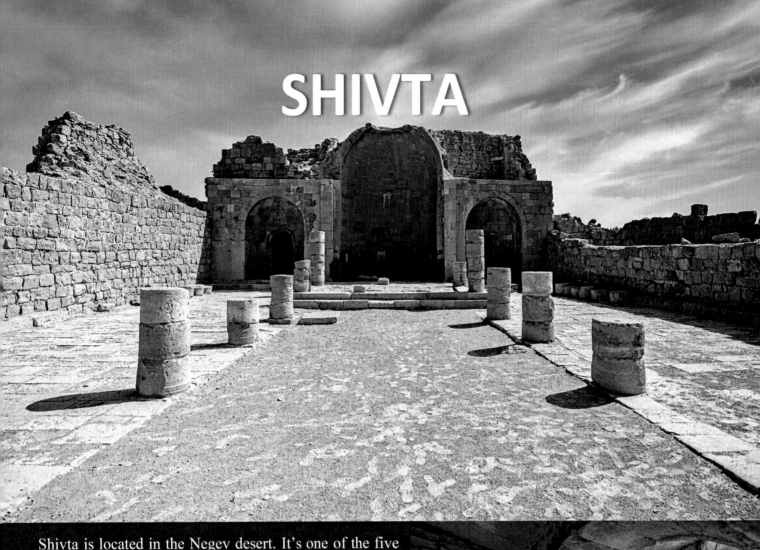

Shivta is located in the Negev desert. It's one of the five Nabatean towns built along the spice route across the desert to the ancient port of Gaza.

Although there was no spring or well nearby to dig for water during the Byzantine period, it was transformed into an oasis as a result of their ingenuity in collecting rain water into reservoirs and cisterns. Water was needed for vineyards, fruit trees, wheat, barley and herding which were common 1.500 years ago.

Water reservoirs and cisterns were incredible accomplishments despite the fact that they had very little rain but flash floods which still occur until this very day.

The exact date of construction is unclear, but based on its pottery, it seems that it was first settled between the end of the 1st C BC to 1st C AD. Most of the infrastructure was built much later from 4th to 5th C AD.

Shivta flourished during the Byzantine-Christian era when its residents accumulated great wealth from the spice route entrepreneurship and served the pilgrims who came to visit their churches and relics. Its first inhabitants were nomads who settled in the area raising camels, goats and sheep. With the advent of Christianity in the region in the 4th C AD, they eventually became Christians and farmers.

Despite the Muslim invasion of the 7th C AD, Shivta continued to exist but after heavy taxes were imposed, the residents gradually left Shivta and by the 9th C AD the area was abandoned. Today we can appreciate: The Stable House, the Pool House, the Pool Square, Three Churches, The Mosque, Look Out, Wine Press and more. Shivta is run by the National Park Authority and is a UNESCO World Heritage site.

SOREQ CAVE

Up until May 1968, no one ever imagined -- even perhaps from the beginning of history -- the magnificent treasure hidden from human eyes. Then by accident, a Stalactites-Stalagmites cave was discovered while quarrying on the western Judean hills.

The cave has a maximum length of 91 m, maximum width of 80 m, maximum height 15 m, with a total of 4.800 square meters. To keep the cave open to the public, it must remain under natural conditions all year round at 22° C and a humidity of 92-100%.

Stalactites are the result of the dissolution and sedimentation of rocks. With the passing of time, in a very slow process water can dissolve the dolomite rock present in that area. Water then expands, dissolving the rock and creating this marvelous natural sculpture.

After the cave was discovered, quarrying nearby was stopped and a decade later it was opened to the public after careful study on how to preserve the cave for future generations.

Great effort and investments were made in order to safeguard and preserve it, though it is a site of minor significance in the Land of the Messiah.

The atmosphere in the cave, level of carbon monoxide, temperature and humidity are continually monitored, even the surrounding area which is the cave's "source of life" -- the seeping rain. Today the Soreg Cave is under the protection of the Nature

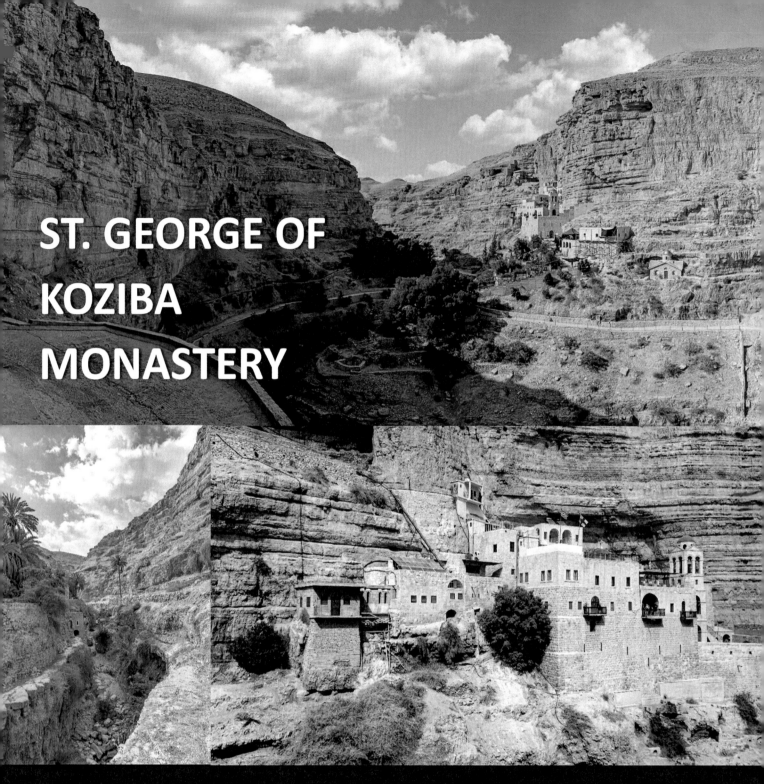

ST. GEORGE OF KOZIBA MONASTERY

Also known as John Jacob of Koziba, it is located in the Judean desert running parallel to the ancient road from Jerusalem to Jericho that inspired Yeshua with His story of the Good Samaritan.

The monastery hanging from the cliff of Wadi Qelt gives a breathtaking view. It started as a Laura in the early 5th C AD with a few monks who sought God and themselves in the desert. They lived in one of the caves which they believed was the cave used by the Prophet Elijah, where he was fed by ravens as he was on his way to the Sinai Peninsula (1 Kings 17:5-6).

Hermits from nearby caves met once a week for prayers and shared meals. By 480 AD, the monastery was founded by John of Thebes who came from Egypt. Tragically, the monastery was destroyed in 614 AD by

However, at the end of the 6ᵗʰ C AD, St. George of Koziba who became the most famous of the monks who lived there and survived the Persian massacre, was forced to live in the ruins of the monastery. The monastery was named in his honor.

In 1179 AD, the monastery was restored by Byzantine King Manuel I Komnenus, but badly damaged again after the Crusaders were expelled from the Holy Land, then fully re-established in 1878 by eastern orthodox Christians who are today the custodians of the place.

Relics of the monks murdered by the Persians are on display. However, depending on the monk or priest looking after the sanctuary, photography is forbidden except in Elijah's cave in the upper area.

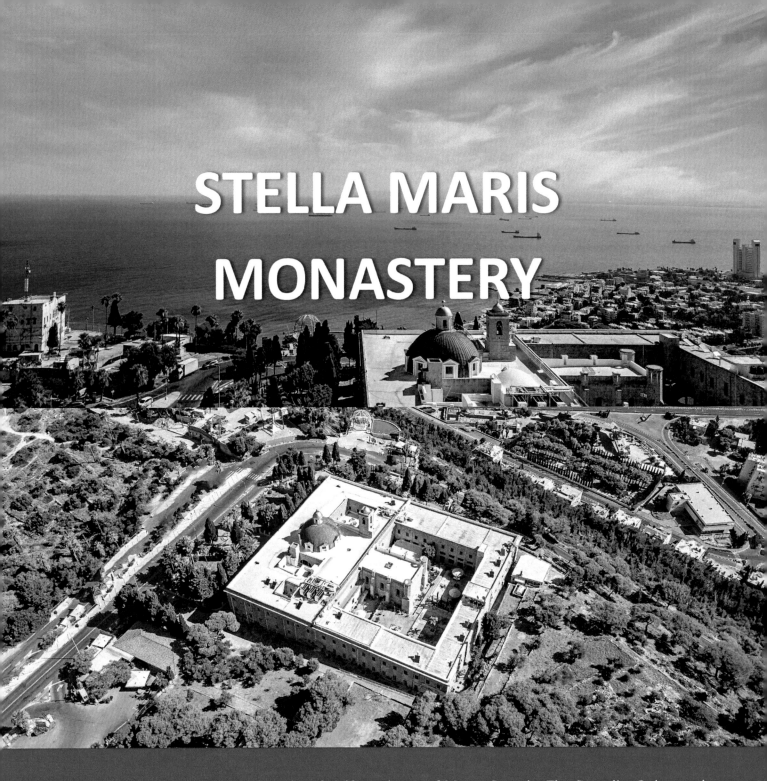

STELLA MARIS MONASTERY

The monastery is located in the modern city of Haifa northwest of Mount Carmel. The Carmelite Order are the custodians of the sanctuary (see Mount Carmel [Mukhraka]).

The original monastery was first built upon a cave which, according to a medieval tradition, was one of the caves used by the prophet Elijah. When the Second Kingdom of Jerusalem fell in 1291 AD, the Carmelites were forced to leave the Holy Land and went to Europe where they flourished but did not forget their origin.

Coming back in 1631 AD, they built a modest monastery close to where the lighthouse stands today. But a century later the independent ruler of Galilee Zahir al-Umir ordered them to leave, then destroyed their monastery.

The monks moved to the present location by first clearing the rubble of the previous church which once stood there above the cave in the Byzantine period.

The church was seriously damaged during Napoleon's campaign in 1799. At the same time Napoleon was defeated in Akko and returned to Europe. His wounded soldiers were left behind and slaughtered by Turkish soldiers, and the monks were evacuated from the monastery for serving them. For this reason, there is a monument in front of the church in honor of the wounded French soldiers who were killed by the Turks while injured and sick.

That was not all. In 1821, Abdulla Pasha of Acre ordered the total destruction of the monastery so it could no longer serve as a refugee camp for his enemies. The masonry was later used to build a summer place which is still standing today and a lighthouse, which the Carmelites bought in 1831, and in 1836 the present church was rebuilt.

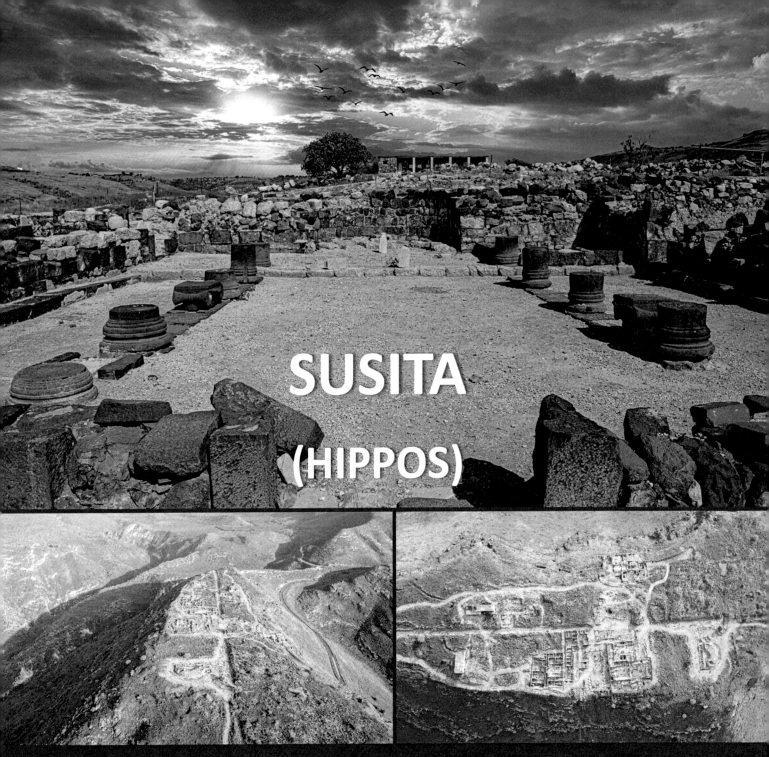

SUSITA

(HIPPOS)

It is one of the Decapolis cities located in the center of the Golan Heights during the Hellenistic, Roman and Byzantine periods, east shore of the Kinneret and basically opposite Tiberias. Today, only two Decapolis cities are in Israel (Beit She'an is the other one) and the rest are in the Hashemite Kingdom of Jordan.

The city was built by the Seleucids at the beginning of the 2nd C BC and named Antiochia-Hippos. It resembles the shape of a horse hence the suffix hippos (horse) was used.

The city lacked water, so water cisterns were built, until eventually water was brought in the Roman period via aqueducts from springs in the Golan Heights.

During the Hasmonean period about 83-80 BC, the city was conquered by Alexander Jannaeus forcing its inhabitants to convert to Judaism or leave the city. Many chose the latter.

This annexation to the new Jewish kingdom did not last long when Pompey came to the Near East in 63 BC conquering the entire Hasmonean kingdom and incorporating it into the Roman Empire. It was then given semi-autonomy as one of the Decapolis cities, though for a brief period it became part of Herod's kingdom as a gift from Augustus Caesar (37-4 BC). After his death the city came under the control of the district of Damascus.

During the Roman period, the city was remodeled and expanded and new public buildings were built. During the Great Revolt 66-73 AD, Hippos was spared since the inhabitants were mostly pagans and indifferent to Jewish nationalism. As the Roman Empire became Christian during the Byzantine period, many churches were built in the city giving it substantial significance.

Despite the conquests that took place in the 7th C AD by the Persians in 614 and then 636 AD, Hippos saw a decline in population even when they were allowed to practice Christianity. However, Hippos came to an end when a major earthquake swept through the Land in 749 AD knocking down its massive pillars and killing many people. The survivors abandoned the place which was never rebuilt.

The place is under the care of National Park Authority and as of the writing of this book, it is open to the public every

SUSYA

Susya is an ancient Jewish town located southeast of Mount Hebron. In biblical times, it would have been on the southern edge of the tribe of Judah, basically at the edge of the Judean desert and had a semi-desert nature.
Since the annual rainfall is low, thousands of water cisterns were dug to compensate its scarcity.

It developed after the second Jewish revolt also known as the Bar-Kokhba revolt in 132-135 AD and it reached its peak between the end of the Byzantine Period and the beginning of the Arab period in the 7th C AD.

What is baffling for historians and archaeologists alike is that despite its size and centrality, Susya was not mentioned by Jewish sources of its time period or even by church father Eusebius in his Onomasticon, perhaps leading us to believe Susya was built after the 5th C AD.

After the destruction of the temple in Jerusalem in 70 AD and its recovery from Yavne, Jewish life became highly community-oriented allowing the population to live in organized towns.

The town demonstrated how well-organized everything was from careful planning to the execution of private dwellings, public buildings, streets, and the water supply system.

We know little of the last stages of Susya or how long the community continued to dwell here including its nature in the Middle Ages with its Muslim rulers. The few pieces of pottery from the Crusader into the Mamluk period seem to indicate a sparse presence in the 13th-14th C AD, therefore, we are not clear of its character during this time period and what brought its final abandonment.

What to see in Susya: The Water Cisterns, Burial cave, Wall houses, Mikveh (purification pools), Dwelling Houses, the Cave of the Arch (dwelling cave), Escape Tunnel, the Olive Press, the Synagogue, and the Public Cave.

TABGHA

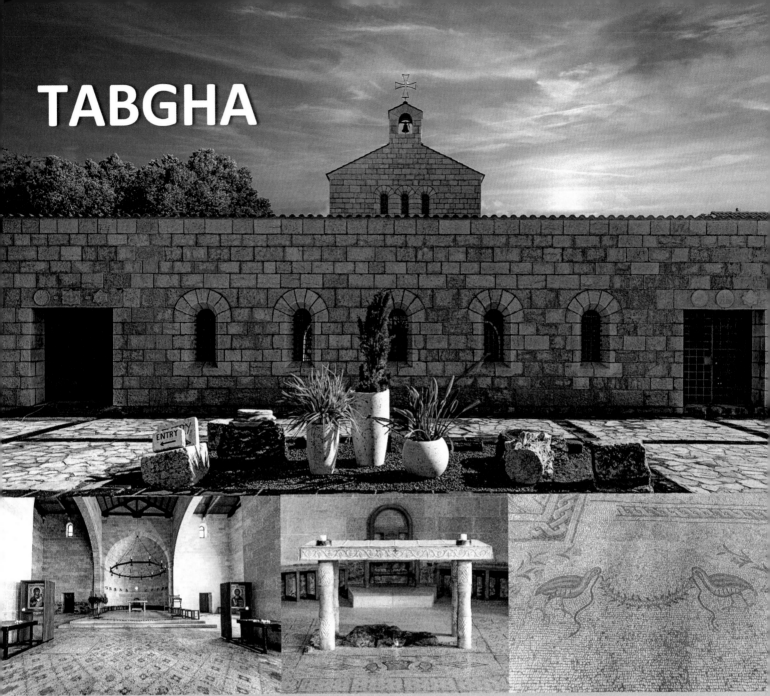

Also known as the Church of the Feeding of the Five Thousand. The word Tabgha is a corruption of the Greek Heptapegon (seven springs) into the Arabic. It is located northwest of the corner of the Kinneret beside the ancient road from Tiberias to Damascus.

We read in Matthew 14:13-21 how Yeshua was able to feed five thousand men, not counting women and children, from five loaves of bread and two fishes. The text does not say that He multiplied the food but rather that He fed them. Antonine Lavoiser, 18th C. scientist discovered that matter cannot be created or destroyed but rather transformed.

But in this case Yeshua defied physics since matter was created with an attribute, we see in Genesis 1:1. In this case, Yeshua is demonstrated to be more than just a teacher or healer but One who can create matter out of nothing. From the little you have; He can make it abundant to allow provision to others.

Early Christians assigned the miracle to the present location along with the Sermon on the Mount and Peter's restoration after the resurrection.

According to Christian tradition, the early followers of Yeshua from Capernaum venerated a large stone that Yeshua used to lay out the bread and fish to feed the five thousand people. The same rock was used as an altar in the center of the first church ever to be built in that location -- right beside the ancient Via Maris by a Judeo-Christian from Tiberias known as St. Josipos.

By the end of the 5th C AD, a Byzantine-style church with a beautifully decorated mosaic floor of heavy Egyptian influence was built on it. The stone, which by this time was reduced in size, was placed under the altar.

During the Persian invasion in 614 AD, the church was destroyed and forgotten until 1932 when it was rediscovered with some of the mosaic surprisingly still intact. In 1980-82 the ancient Byzantine Basilica was rebuilt and is managed by the Benedictine Order.

TEL ARAD

The site is located in the southern border of the Judean desert dating back as early as the Chalcolithic Age to the Byzantine period.

During the Chalcolithic period (about 4000-3400 BC) the settlement was not walled, though that was not the case during a later period within the early Bronze Age (ca 2900-2700 BC), when a large city was built upon the previous settlement with a thick wall (almost 2 m thick) towering along its length. It was a prosperous city located at the intersection of trade routes. It was a well-planned city with a temple.

Numbers 21:1 and 33:40 mention that Hebrews from Egypt were prevented from passing through this territory, though eventually they defeated them according to the account of Joshua 12:7 and 14.

Scholars today ask if Tel Arad is actually Canaanite Arad (Hormah) since no Late Bronze Age layers were found here -- the time of the coming of the Israelites. It is suggested that biblical Arad was an area rather than a specific city and Hormah was in a different location. The Israelite period dates from the Iron Age (11th C BC), which was a fortress on the summit of the Tel. It has protecting walls and tower and is the only surviving Israelite temple with an altar, a holy place, holy of holiest and replicas of Matsevot (standing stones) representing deities, in this case the God of Israel and

The presence of this temple has caused tremendous theological problems and implications. The soldiers deployed in this remote place were worshiping the God of Israel and His Ashera or consort.
Only Jerusalem was the place to worship and offer sacrifices to the God of the Israelites, but Arad was not the only place in such a dilemma – Be'er Sheva and Lachish as well.

What brought the worship of the God of the Hebrews to an end in Arad? The standing stones showed signs of violence. Was this the result of the so-called "Hezekiah reformation" or was it a foreign force stronger than the Judean King?

Certainly, the Assyrians had a lot to do with the destruction of the Judean towns and villages including this one. When Hezekiah decided to rebel in 701 BC, King Sennacherib came with his army like locusts not just to get paid but to vent his anger. They destroyed this site and looted the temples to demonstrate the sovereignty of the Assyrian gods over the gods of those whom they conquered.

The area was re-used during the Hellenistic, Hasmonean, Roman and Byzantine periods.
When visiting the area remember that when the Canaanite city was active, the Israelites were not yet in possession. And when the Israelite fortress functioned thereafter, the Canaanite city was long gone.
Today Tel Arad is managed by the National Park Authority.

TEL AZEKA

The Tel is located between the Elah stream (valley) and Azeka junction with the road leading to Beit Shemesh, the area is known as the Shephelah or lowland.

Based on archaeological excavations carried out at the beginning of the 20th C, the material culture found on site indicates habitation since the Second Millennium BC (ca 1900 BC).

Its first biblical account comes from the pages of the Book of Joshua on the conquest of the Land by the Israelites (Joshua 10:10-11) and it was given to the tribe of Judah (Joshua 15:20, 35-36).

Between the 11th - 8th C BC, it was under the control of the Judean kings marking a territorial border with the Philistines who were nearby.

One of the most remembered biblical battles took place in the valley of Elah. The Philistines came to challenge the forces of King Saul and none was brave enough to fight the intimidating man from Gath – Goliath. And David, being just a young lad and shepherd but with unshakable trust and assurance in the God of Israel, came forward and slew the giant, stirring confidence in the rest of the Israelite soldiers by chasing away their enemies.

In 701 BC, it was among the 46 cities that the Assyrian King Sennacherib conquered in Judea after his father took control of the northern kingdom and made Judah a vessel of the Assyrians.

After the Assyrians were conquered by the Babylonians and subsequently the Babylonians by the Persians in 539 BC, King Cyrus allowed those who were in exile to return to their home lands.

Many of them did so, like Ezrah and Nehemiah, among others (Nehemiah 11:1, 30). Azeka and other towns were rebuilt but still under the rule of the Persians.

During the late Roman period, Azeka was destroyed again by the Romans due to the Bar Kokhba revolt in 132-135 AD.

Church father Eusebius of Caesarea in his book Onomasticon stated that Azeka was known as Kefar Zechariah in the Byzantine period. It was abandoned and has lain in ruins until today.

As of the writing of this book, the site is still being excavated by archaeologists and is under the supervision of the National Park Authority. It is open to the public free of charge. The view of the Elah valley from the top gives us a better perspective of the location of the Israelites and the Philistines when they confronted each other.

TEL BE'ER SHEVA

Tel Be'er Sheva valley and Arad valley are identified with the biblical Negev of Judah. In the past due to the stream beds that served as passageways, early dwellers chose the area to settle in, allowing them to dig wells for themselves, their agriculture and for grazing animals.

Although the site bears the name Sheva or Be'er Sheva, it was not the one where the Patriarchs (Abraham, Isaac and Jacob) lived. However, it became known later on as the southern border of the Judean kingdom.

The site was inhabited on and off for thousands of years from as early as the Chalcolithic period 4th Millennium BC. The following settlement was in the early Iron Age 12th C BC leaving a huge gap of over two thousand years (i.e., the Bronze Age). By the 10th C BC, it was an enclosed settlement until eventually it became an administrative city. Under the Judean kings, it began to see technological advancement of its period, such as a glacis for defense, thick casemate walls, and a well built underground water cistern.

The most remarkable yet theologically controversial find was a well-preserved Israelite altar with all the paraphernalia such as stone incense, female figurines, etc. The altar is displayed in the Israel Museum in Jerusalem.
One may ask how can this be even possible when the only place for burning incense and offering sacrifices was in Jerusalem? This was not only the case during this time period in Tel Be'er Sheva, but in Arad and Lachish as well since altars and shrines were found in all of these three locations.

The so-called Hezekiah or Josiah reform was perhaps more of a local reform than a major national reform.
The evidence on the ground shows that these practices continued all the way to 8th C BC when the Assyrians destroyed at least forty towns of Judah and carried the spoils from their cities (see Lachish).

The site was occupied again during the Persian period 5th-4th C BC but just as a fortress, later on during the Hellenistic period in 3rd-2nd C BC a temple was built on top of it.

During the Herodian 1st C BC-1st C AD, Roman 2nd-3rd C AD and early Arab periods 7th- 8th C AD, the site was used as a fortress also.
What to see: A replica of the Israelite altar, the Outer Gate, the Well, the Drainage Channel, the Main Gate, the City Square, the "Governor's Palace", Residential Quarter, the Casemate Wall; the Water System, among others.
Tel Be'er Sheva besides being a National Park well deserves the title of World Heritage site by UNESCO.

TEL DAN

When coming to visit the site, one cannot believe that this is in the Middle East, especially as this Land is 60% desert. It is like stepping into a mini forest with such a wide variety of flora and fauna in just 120 acres.

The Dan spring is the richest of the three rivers feeding the Jordan River. No wonder the first settlers in the area decided to come there about 7.000 years ago.

By the Middle of the Bronze Age (2700-2400 BC), a well-fortified city built on glacis surrounded the area. It was known as Laish, which was later taken by the tribe of Dan who struggled against the Philistines to gain control over their given area.

By default, Dan became the northernmost border of the Kingdom of Israel and the first to be conquered by the Northern powers.

According to the Book of Genesis, Abraham overcame the five kings in Laish (Genesis 14:14).
During the Israelite period the city was reinforced and fortified in the 9th - 8th C BC. Sections are still visible today such as walls, gates and streets.

The major discovery of this site was what is known as Abraham's Arch dating from the Middle Bronze Age. This made it the oldest in the world, or at least competing with Ashkelon's arch. The base of the altar and platform were built by Jeroboam. Significantly, no temple has been found beside the altar, platform (bima) and other cultic objects as of the writing of this book.

Another major discovery was a tablet with a carved inscription by King Hazael of Damascus boasting of his victory over Israel and the kings of the house of David. This was the first time the house of David was mentioned outside of the Bible. It is displayed today at the Israel Museum in Jerusalem.

Besides a beautiful hike in the Nature Reserve, other things to see are the: Wading Pool, the Pistachio Lookout, Pooh Bear's Tree, the Dan Spring, "The Garden of Eden", the Canaanite Gate, and Israelite Gate. Dan fell into Assyrian hands in the 8th C BC and was later re-inhabited until the Roman era when the people moved close to Banias and the area was abandoned.

Today Dan is run by the Nature Reserve Authority.

TEL REHOV

One of the largest Canaanite-Israelite sites found in the country today. Inhabited for hundreds of years during both the Middle Bronze Age and the Israelite period, it is located in the Jordan Valley near the ancient city of Beit She'an. Today agricultural fields surround the site.

The city was well known during the Bronze Age, and is mentioned in Egyptian records such as the Stela of Pharaoh Seti I 14th-13th C BC.

Its impressive findings are displayed today at the Israel Museum in Jerusalem. The largest mosaic floor of an ancient Synagogue from the 6th C AD and an apiary (the largest known in the Middle East from the 10th C BC) where they manufactured bees' honey were uncovered.

A piece of broken sherd (clay) with the name 'Elisha' was found from the 9th C BC, the same time period as the Prophet Elisha, disciple of the famous Prophet Elijah. However, Professor Amihai Mazar, one of the leading archaeologists from the Hebrew University, could not confirm this 'Elisha'.

Nonetheless, Dr. Stephen Pfann from the University of the Holy Land noted that 'Elisha' was not a common name in this time period and therefore concluded that the name on the piece of pottery does indeed refer to the Prophet Elisha.

The evidence between Tel Rehov and the Prophet Elisha is still far from conclusive. As of the writing of this book, the area is now neglected and the mud bricks have become birds' nests, destroying the walls. We hope one day the National Park Authority will protect the area. It is open with no supervision.

TEL YIZREEL

After the split in the Kingdom of Solomon at the end of the 10th C BC, the Kingdom of Israel was divided between north and south -- or between the Kingdom of Israel (north) and Judah (south). Yizreel (Jezreel) was a major city during the period of the Northern kingdom 9th C BC when it became the capital. It is located on a hill on the western edge of the Gilboa Mountains. The city was connected to the center of the country towards Jerusalem (today via Jenin) and access to the major Yizreel valley -- basically the gatekeeper to these major trading routes.

Due to its location, the city was already inhabited during the Canaanite period starting from around the 15th C BC to the Iron Age/Israelite period. The Northern kingdom enjoyed a prosperous period and the material culture and fortification found in Hazor, Jezreel, Megiddo and Rehov can testify to such affluence. However, like everything in life, it came to an end, starting with the first Assyrian invasion in 732 BC. In the Hellenistic, Hasmonean, Roman and Byzantine periods, the city was restored. And during the time of the ministry of Yeshua, it was one of the routes He took to go to Jerusalem via Samaria. By the Crusader and Ottoman periods, Yizreel was a small village and its remains are still visible today. As of the writing of this book, the site is still being excavated and it is open to the public for free.

TIMNA PARK

Timna possessed the oldest copper mine in the world beginning over 6.000 years ago, basically the period when humans acquired the skill of using copper or any other metal. For the ancient world this was a revolutionary technological advancement. People began using copper on a daily basis.

The Egyptians were entrepreneurs when they began abstracting the copper in this area around 14th-12th C BC from the reign of Seti I - Ramses V. However, they were not alone in this revolutionary lucrative business -- the Medianites, Kenites and those from the Arabian Peninsula also entered into the partnership.

The copper was transported all the way to the gulf of Eilat and from there to Egypt via the Red Sea. The mines were later abandoned though more mining was carried on in the 10th C BC presumably during the reign of King Solomon, but not as much as was done in the mines of Funon in the Transjordan. It resumed during the

Timna Park is located in the Arabah desert a few kilometers north of the city of Eilat. With its combination of stunning scenery and incredible history, it truly makes the site very enjoyable, not just for tourists but for locals alike.

In addition to the ancient copper mines from different time periods, material culture left behind by the miners includes ruins of the temple of Hathor, the goddess of the miners, Graffiti of the Chariots, hunters with bows and arrows and animals, and wall drawing of Ramses III offering gifts to the god of Hathor.

Also, there are natural sculptures as a result of erosion such as the Mushroom, the Arches, and the so called "Solomon's Pillar" -- creating red canyons so majestic and amusing to look at.

Beside natural beauty, visitors can try mountain biking, boat riding on the artificial lake, or even overnight camping.

You can also enjoy a replica of the Tabernacle based on the measurements and ordinances given to Moses during their journey through the desert (Exodus 25).

YEHIAM FORTRESS

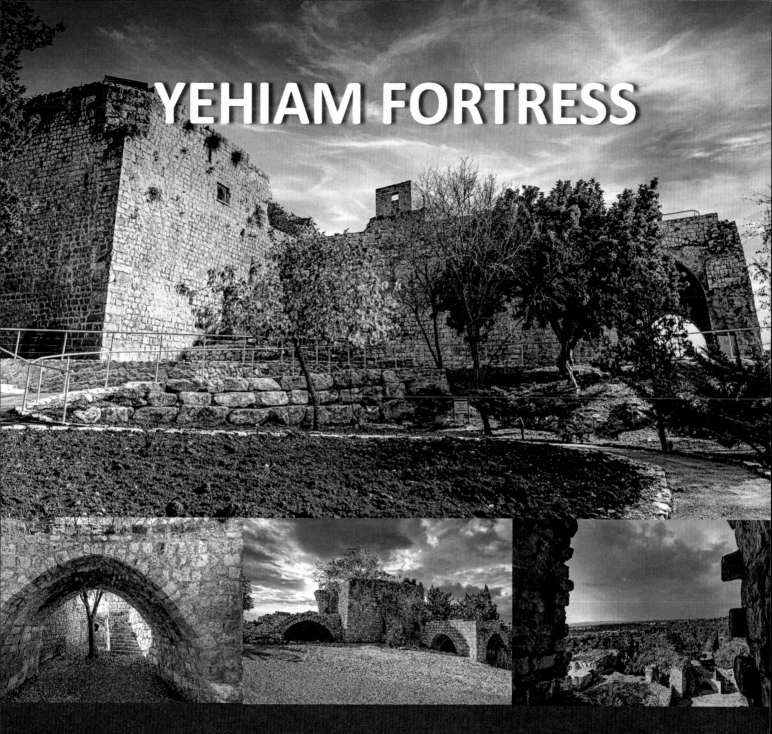

Yehiam fortress is a typical example of how throughout the ages a place has been re-used for the same purpose, which is not unique since we see this phenomenon all over the Land.

From the Romans to the Byzantines, to the Crusaders and all the way to the Ottomans, the site was used as a strategic place overlooking the coastal plain, preventing access by invaders, and protecting the passage to Upper Galilee. However, during the Crusader period, it was used in the Second Crusaders kingdom (i.e., Akko) to protect the capital from invaders coming from the east, especially when they lost during the Battle of Hattin in 1187 AD and as a result were left with part of Galilee and the coastal plain.

As of the writing of this book, the entire fortress has not yet been studied in depth, so who knows what is yet to be discovered or learned from it.

The Byzantines built and fortified a farming community of monks. The Crusader period left typical elongated vaults and towers with looped holes where they could shoot at their enemies. They also established this farming system throughout Galilee, some under private family owners or sold to different orders within the Crusaders kingdom, in this case the Teutonic Order. When they strengthened the tower's defense system, they named it Judin.

Despite their well-fortified defense system, it did not prevent it from destruction under the command of Sultan Baibars.

In the 18th C AD Sheik Mahd el-Hussein became the local ruler of Galilee and partially rebuilt the fortress. But in 1738 Dahr el-Ommar, a Bedouin, gained control of Galilee and took the fortress for himself.

The main section of what we see today dates from that time period. Dahr el-Ommar's rule came to an end after the Turks had had enough of his rebellion and self-appointed ruling of Galilee; hence he was killed in a battle in Akko in 1775 AD.

The National Park Authority carried out major reconstruction and safeguarded the fortress. When visiting the site do not forget to go to the top to see its surrounding area and understand why they chose to build on this exact location over and over again.

Around the fortress, the trenches from the 1948 Israel War of Independence are still visible and can be visited.

ZIPPORI

In the 18th C AD, Daher el-Ommar, the Bedouin ruler of Galilee, fortified Saffuriyyeh which in 1948 housed Arab gangs that acted against the Jewish population during the Israel War of Independence. Eventually they were conquered by the Israelis and decades later it became a National Park.

When visiting, see: The ancient Water Reservoir, the Masha pool, the street network, the Nile House, the Western Church and Orpheus House, the Dionysus House (the beautiful woman known as the Monalisa of Galilee), the fortress, the Roman Theater, among others.

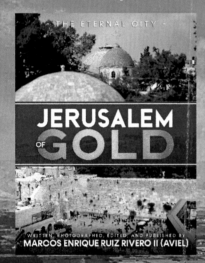